JOHN SEARLE

Continuum Contemporary American Thinkers

The Continuum Contemporary American Thinkers series offers concise and accessible introductions to the most important and influential thinkers at work in philosophy today. Designed specifically to meet the needs of students and readers encountering these thinkers for the first time, these informative books provide a coherent overview and analysis of each thinker's vital contribution to the field of philosophy. The series is the ideal companion to the study of these most inspiring and challenging of thinkers

Daniel Dennett, David L. Thompson
Hilary Putnam, Lance P. Hickey
Saul Kripke, Arif Ahmed

JOHN SEARLE

JOSHUA RUST

continuum

Continuum International Publishing Group
The Tower Building   80 Maiden Lane
11 York Road   Suite 704
London SE1 7NX   New York NY 10038

www.continuumbooks.com

British Library Cataloguing-in-Publication Data
A catalogue record for this book is available from the British Library.

ISBN: HB: 978-0-8264-9751-2
         PB: 978-0-8264-9752-9

Library of Congress Cataloging-in-Publication Data
Rust, Joshua.
John Searle / Joshua Rust.
p. cm.
ISBN-13: 978-0-8264-9751-2 (HB)
ISBN-10: 0-8264-9751-9 (HB)
ISBN-13: 978-0-8264-9752-9 (pbk.)
ISBN-10: 0-8264-9752-7 (pbk.)
1. Searle, John R. I. Title.
B1649.S264R87 2009
191–dc22
2009005987

Typeset by Newgen Imaging Systems Pvt Ltd, Chennai, India
Printed and bound in Great Britain by MPG Books Ltd,
Bodmin, Cornwall

For my mother, father, Dan, and Jon

CONTENTS

ACKNOWLEDGEMENTS

Thanks to those who students participated in my seminar on John Searle at Stetson University in the fall of 2008. Special thanks to my colleagues at Stetson, Ronald Hall and Susan Peppers-Bates, and to those who helped me edit the manuscript, including Kim Bowen and especially Marijana Weiner.

Joshua Rust, Stetson University

INTRODUCTION

Philosopher David Papineau writes of John R. Searle, "Whenever he is faced with a conflict between common sense and arcane philosophical doctrine, he backs common sense every time."[1] While common sense would have us take science seriously, for Searle that commitment must be reconciled with an equally profound commitment to, for example, the reality of our mental lives or the experience of our acting freely. Searle challenges, with the zeal of a journalistic muckraker, those philosophers who would deny these mundane features of our lived experience. His prose is scrappy and clear, pulsing with intellectual joy. In the introduction to *Intentionality*, Searle writes, "Where questions of style and exposition are concerned I try to follow a simple maxim: if you can't say it clearly you don't understand it yourself."[2] His defense of common sense is coupled with a no-nonsense approach to the exhibition and resolution of philosophical quandaries.

Searle was born in Denver, Colorado, in 1932 to a mother who was a medical doctor and a father who was an electrical engineer. He attended an experimental John Dewey High School in New York before graduating from Shorewood High School in Wisconsin. As a college student he attended the University of Wisconsin before pursuing a graduate degree at Oxford, where he studied with John Austin, Peter Strawson, and Jim Urmson. Over the course of his seven years at Oxford he received both his B. A. and Ph. D. in philosophy. He met his wife, Dagmar, in Austin's office, while he was a research lecturer at Christ College. In 1959, it was Austin who helped him get an assistant professorship at the University of California at Berkeley. Today he is the Mills Professor of Philosophy of Mind and Language at that same institution.

The breadth of John Searle's corpus is astonishing. Any treatment of his output faces the challenge of bringing a varied set of topics under a coherent narrative. To date, overviews of Searle's work tend to track his intellectual development—beginning with the philosophy of language, moving to the philosophy of mind, and concluding with his investigation into institutional reality. This sequence is shaped by factors besides that of intellectual perspicuity, including Searle's responsiveness to a changing philosophical climate.

However, this book proceeds conceptually,[3] rather than chronologically, beginning with an investigation into the most general features of Searle's ontological and methodological commitments.

Chapter 1 outlines Searle's metaphysical framework. There is one world, independent of us, consisting of particles in fields of force. A philosophical question typically concerns the status of facts that are not easily reconcilable with this basic ontology: subjective qualitative experience, intentional mental states, actions, rationality, freedom, language, and social reality. Searle's *questions*, at least as articulated in the latter half of his career,[4] are roughly those asked by Scientific Naturalists—metaphysicians working in the twilight of the linguistic turn.

What distinguishes Searle from many of his intellectual peers, then, are the answers he gives to these questions, the methods by which he generates these answers, and their broad scope. The keystone of Searle's philosophical program lies in the notion of intentionality. Searle's central task involves reconciling mind with body; he has to show that intentionality is not at odds with his ontological commitment to Scientific Naturalism. Chapters 2 and 3 review this attempt.

Once a naturalized notion of intentionality is in hand, Searle is in a position to resolve a number of otherwise pressing philosophical problems. Chapter 4 looks at the way his notion of intentionality can be used to distinguish action from mere behavior. Similarly, Chapters 5, 6, and 7 display the way in which Searle leverages certain properties of an intentional state to helpfully account for speech actions, without collapsing the latter into mere actions, or cases of natural meaning, or blind causal processes. Finally Chapters 8 and 9 show how speech acts are a special case of institutional phenomena in general. Thus, the explanatory strategies employed in accounting for meaning can be generalized to account for a variety of socially constructed facts.

While this text is primarily exegetical, some critical assessment of Searle's views can be found in the final three chapters.

CHAPTER 1

FUNDAMENTAL ONTOLOGY: EXTERNAL REALISM AND SCIENTIFIC NATURALISM

Bumping around in the world as we do, we develop certain expectations about how things work. After not having eaten for several hours, I expect to be hungry. I expect no cross traffic when the signal is green. Upon picking up a ringing phone, I expect there to be someone on the line. These expectations are based on real, but not indelible patterns; they are, moreover, entrenched, so that their violation might prompt genuine surprise and puzzlement. I have not eaten in eight hours—why am I not hungry? Did the other driver not see the red light? Why did the phone ring?

These expectations develop quite naturally as a person comes to have more and more experience with the world. But other expectations become entrenched as the result of systematic inquiry. Chemists recently discovered that the limestone blocks which constitute the Pyramids at Giza exhibit surprising chemical structures: observed traces of rapid chemical reaction, in place of natural crystallization, are incomprehensible if the stones were quarried (given the chemical theories that account for the development of these stones).[1] No natural limestone has been discovered that exhibits the microproperties found in at least some of the blocks that compose the pyramids; they contain, for example, an unusual amount of silicon. These particular blocks also uniformly exhibit a higher mass on one side and air bubbles near the other. What explains these anomalies? A background theory, and the expectations it implies, are conditions against which requests for explanation gain traction.[2] If these blocks were poured from a limestone concrete solution, rather than quarried, these properties are explicable. This study concludes that many of the pyramid's blocks appear, not to be cut, but formed from a kind of limestone cement.

Philosophers, including Searle, are likewise in the business of both recognizing and resolving puzzles. Philosophical puzzles are explanatory puzzles, and so imply a background theory against which certain phenomena come to appear as anomalous. If chemical and geological theories give rise to puzzlement concerning the microstructure of certain blocks found in the Giza pyramids, Searle wonders how certain phenomena—including meaning and consciousness—are likewise compatible with the findings of science. Searle opens his book, *The Construction of Social Reality*, with a general claim about the kinds of philosophical problems that interest him.

> We live in exactly one world, not two or three or seventeen. As far as we currently know, the most fundamental features of that world are as described by physics, chemistry, and the other natural sciences. But the existence of phenomena that are not in any obvious way physical or chemical gives rise to puzzlement. How, for example, can there be states of consciousness or meaningful speech acts as parts of the physical world? Many of the philosophical problems that most interest me have to do with how the various parts of the world relate to each other—how does it all hang together?—and much of my work in philosophy has been addressed to these questions.[3]

Just as an absence of crystallization in certain limestone blocks defies expectations codified in chemical theory, the philosophical puzzles that interest Searle gain traction against his strong endorsement of a scientific metaphysics. The chemists did not conclude that these anomalous chemical configurations falsify chemical theory; rather, they told a story about how these traces could be rendered compatible with our current scientific theories. The story is that the blocks were poured, not quarried. Chemical theory is part of the theoretical base against which scientific problems are identified. This base consists of a set of theories or paradigms that embody a shared set of empirical expectations. Similarly, to Searle's eye, the presence of language and consciousness seems prima facie incompatible with the world as construed by the natural sciences. And Searle, like the chemists, wants to tell a story about how one can endorse the scientific outlook while simultaneously accounting for these philosophical anomalies. In short, he wants to explain how it all hangs together.

EXTERNAL REALISM

We access the world by way of mental representation—visual perception, touch, taste, sound, and smell. We might say that our experience of the world is always mediated by a cognitive apparatus. What explains these conscious experiences and representations?

On the one hand, realists, including Searle, want to say that these experiences are caused by an external reality which is logically independent of those experiences and representations.

On the other hand, skeptics and idealists see no independent evidence for a reality that exists independent of our mental states. If all of our experiences are mediated, it seems irresponsible to posit an additional, representation-independent world. We smile when we see a cat at the side of a television, intent on catching the object which disappeared off the side of the screen. We of course understand that there is nothing behind the representation on the screen—at least nothing like the object displayed. Similarly, a skeptic might contend that there is nothing independent of the wall of representation which constitutes our experience. They might observe with amusement the realist's pawing for a world claimed to exist independently of anyone's experience.

Searle vehemently disagrees with this view, whose supporters include Bishop Berkeley. Berkeley writes "All the choir of heaven and furniture of the earth, in a word all those bodies which compose the mighty frame of the world, have not any subsistence without a mind."[4] Bertrand Russell is also among Searle's targets. Scientific truths are not, according to Russell, basic truths; they are rather simply configurations of conscious experience or sense-data. As such, Russell treats the external world as a kind of postulation—a "logical fiction" or a paraphrase of a series of phenomenological experiences bound by relations of similarity and continuous change.[5]

Searle retorts: the fact that the world is mediated by a cognitive apparatus (an epistemic point) need not imply that the world itself is somehow logically dependent on those experiences (a metaphysical point). The existence of the universe does not depend on the experience of any being within that universe. Or, as Searle has it, "there is a real world that exists completely independent of us, that doesn't give a damn about us."[6] He calls this view "External Realism."

While External Realism is intuitively compelling, Searle also recognizes that it is impossible to verify empirically. We can corroborate empirical claims by citing independent evidence for their truth. Both a tripped circuit breaker and a general power outage might explain why the electricity suddenly cut off in my apartment, but only the second explanation explains why my neighbors are also without power. Only a general power outage can explain this independent fact. We saw this in the pyramid example. The lack of a crystalline structure in certain limestone blocks is already strong evidence that the blocks were poured rather than quarried. But this alone is inconclusive. The further fact that they exhibit a certain density profile corroborates this conclusion. However, the more global claim that there persists a reality which is independent of our representations cannot be corroborated in this way; the very terms in which the question is phrased precludes some sort of independent verification.

We have conscious experience. What explains this experience? External Realists want to posit a representation-independent reality as a significant part of the explanation. But because both realists and skeptics agree that access to this putative reality would anyway be mediated by consciousness, skeptics see no corroborating evidence for External Realism. There is, in short, no way to get behind our experience so as to independently demonstrate an autonomous, physical world.

Searle wants to argue for the existence of a mind-independent reality. But such a reality cannot be treated as just another factual claim, along the lines of the poured limestone blocks. Searle thus offers a transcendental argument for the existence of a mind-independent reality.[7] Transcendental arguments argue back from a factual conviction to its preconditions. He argues, in short, that in communicating factual claims we are *already presupposing* the existence of a mind-independent reality.

More specifically, the idea seems to be as follows: Assertions can be true or false. (1) "Pyramid blocks have a peculiar microphysical structure" and (2) "The world exists independently of our representations" *seem* to be two instances of assertion. Thus, without evidence to the contrary, the idealist or skeptic might be justified in thinking that (2) is false just as further inquiry might lead one to discover (1) to be false. Searle's response is to deny that, in spite of appearances, (2) is a case of genuine assertion. "Rather, (2) is a *presupposition* of (1). Additionally, (2) is a presupposition of other assertions about publically accessible phenomena." If such assertions are true and false, there has to be something about which they are true or false. And whatever this is must be independent of our representations—thinking something does not normally make it so. This is the sense in which (2) is presupposed by any normal understanding of assertions such as (1). Searle says,

> Any truth claim presupposes that there is a way that things are regarding the content of that claim. And this point holds as much for mathematical statements such as "2 + 2 = 4" or for statements about personal experiences such as "I am in pain" as it does for statements about mountains, dogs, and electrons. What is special about these latter sorts of statements is that they purport to make reference to publicly accessible phenomena, in these examples, publicly accessible physical objects. But for such cases we presuppose not only that there is a way that things are that is independent of our representations, but that *there is a way that things are in a publicly accessible, i.e., ontologically objective, realm.*[8]

Moreover, not only does the content of certain assertions presuppose External Realism, the very fact that in asserting we are also communicating also presupposes an external reality in which the hearer exists. If I am a skeptic, with whom am I communicating?

In response, the skeptic could agree that parts of our language seem to presuppose External Realism, but conclude this only implies that these concepts stand in need of conceptual revision. We have, along these lines, come to accept that the objects that we have called "solid" are, in some sense, porous—the atoms which compose them are separated by fields of force.

Searle grants his argument is not conclusive. But if we endorse the skeptic's argument, we are forced to reconfigure our understanding, not just of the concept *solid*, but any utterance which refers to a mind-independent world (Russell attempted something like this). Moreover, we are forced to abandon any ordinary understanding of what it is to communicate with *others*.

Before moving on to Searle's substantive articulation of the nature of external reality, it is worth saying something about the tradition which precedes Searle's articulation of this argument. These admittedly cryptic remarks are intended to give the reader only a taste of a much larger dialogue in which Searle is a participant. The first transcendental argument against the skeptic was advanced by Immanuel Kant in the Refutation of Idealism. Kant argues that an external reality is a condition for the possibility of self-consciousness or "empirical apperception." Undermining the very possibility of skepticism, Kant, unlike Searle, understands his argument to be conclusive. But, for Kant, there remains a sense in which empirical reality is held to be dependent on our cognitive faculties (it is mind-dependent), and so does not satisfy the requirements of External Realism.[9] While Searle's argument bears some affinity to that of G. E. Moore's,[10] Searle explicitly rebukes Moore's argument.[11] Moore offers an argument for the truth of a specific empirical claim, "that [my] two human hands exist." But Searle's argument, unlike Moore's, does not infer the external world from the truth of a particular empirical claim. Rather, Searle argues that statement making of any kind already implies the existence of an external world. Like Kant, Ludwig Wittgenstein's[12] attack on skepticism appears to be more ambitious than Searle's. Searle worries that in adopting the skeptic's conclusion we will be driven to a very foreign interpretation of otherwise perfectly intelligible speech acts. But where Searle only holds that the skeptic must radically alter our normal understanding of the words we say, Wittgenstein makes the stronger claim that skepticism undermines our ability to understand anything whatsoever.

SCIENTIFIC NATURALISM

In the previous section we rehearsed Searle's transcendental argument against the skeptics and idealists who would deny a representation-independent reality. But External Realism makes only a negative claim—if Searle is right, we know that reality, whatever it is, is *not* mind-dependent. Searle also makes a positive claim about the ultimate nature of that external reality.

Searle's fundamental ontology is that of the Scientific Naturalist,[13] in that, not only is the universe representation-independent, but he supposes it to be roughly as the natural sciences describe it as being.[14] Obviously, we will come to discover that some of our scientific theories are in fact false. But the Scientific Naturalist maintains that the basic portrait of the universe as painted by the natural sciences is largely correct, even if there is some disagreement over the details. Searle starkly asserts, "It is a condition of your being an educated person in our era that you are apprised of these two theories: the atomic theory of matter and the evolutionary theory of biology."[15] In particular, the universe consists of subatomic particles in fields of force. These particles are organized into physical, chemical, and biological systems. The development of the biological systems is largely governed by evolutionary processes.

Searle's commitment to Scientific Naturalism is *issue framing* in the sense that this naturalistic fundamental ontology determines what is to count as a philosophical problem. In this respect, Searle is an exemplar of a certain way of doing philosophy. Moreover, it is not unfair to say that this way of doing philosophy has increasingly come to dominate the philosophical imagination since 1950.[16]

By way of locating Searle's work within its historical context, we might start with Wilfrid Sellars' 1962 essay, "Philosophy and the Scientific Image of Man."[17] According to Sellars, philosophical problems are versions of what might be called the *two-images problem*. On the one hand, there is the "manifest image," which is the world as it is ordinarily experienced by human beings. This is a world which is *felt*—conscious agents apprehend macrophysical objects from a first-personal, subjective point of view. That world is moreover filtered through a network of emotions, values, and teleological commitments. On the other hand, there is the "scientific image," which is the world as described by the natural sciences in general, and a mathematized physics in particular. This is the view from nowhere. This world is construed as mechanistic and is free from values and perspectives. The scientific image is compositional in that the behavior of macroconstituents is assumed to be entirely governed by the behavior of microconstituents.

The two-images problem is simply that many features of the manifest image seem irreconcilable with the scientific image. There is, for example, no place for love, or consciousness, in a physicalist ontology of objects being pushed around by blind forces.

In his recent book, *From Ethics to Metaphysics*, Frank Jackson rearticulates the two-images problem under the heading, "the location problem":

> By serious metaphysics, I mean metaphysics . . . that acknowledges that we can do better than draw up big lists, that seeks comprehension in terms of a more or less limited number of ingredients, or anyway a smaller list than we started with. . . . Thus, by its very nature, serious metaphysics continually faces the location problem. Because the ingredients are limited, some putative features of the world are not going to appear *explicitly* in some more basic account. The question then is whether they nevertheless figure implicitly in the more basic account, or whether we should say that to accept that the account is complete, or is complete with respect to some subject-matter or other, commits us to holding that the putative features are *merely* putative.[18]

What Jackson calls the purported or "putative features of the world" correspond to Sellars' manifest image. Philosophers address the two-images or location problem when they try to account for the supposed, putative, manifest image within the framework of the more basic, scientific image. Sometimes, Jackson suggests, this translation will involve the elimination of the putative features (i.e., are shown to be "*merely* putative").

In facing the two-images or location problem, it will be clear that Searle is less tempted than is Jackson by the eliminativist solution. Nevertheless it is important to see that Searle endorses Sellars' and Jackson's formulation of the problem:

> The overriding question in contemporary philosophy is as follows: We now have a reasonably well-established conception of the basic structure of the universe. But it is not at all easy to reconcile the basic facts we have come to know with a certain conception we have of ourselves, derived in part from our cultural inheritance but mostly from our own experience.[19]

The characteristic logical structure of persistent philosophical problems is captured by the two-images or location problem, where putative, manifest features of our experience must be brought into accord with the basic, scientific features of the world. This theoretical base is, for Searle, Sellars, and Jackson, given to us by the physical sciences, which construes the world as a blind, valueless, deterministic, spatiotemporal manifold. These philosophers are Scientific Naturalists, and this is the sense in which Searle agrees that "philosophy starts from the facts of science."[20] It is against the assumption that the world is roughly as science describes it as being, that Searle asks, "How do we fit in?"[21]

Just as the lack of a crystalline structure in certain blocks of the Giza pyramids is baffling only against a set of chemical and geological background theories, for Searle requests for philosophical explanation presuppose the expectations embodied in the metaphysics of Scientific Naturalism. Puzzles, such as the problem of free will and the mind-body problem, arise against the expectation that the world is as science says that it is.

CONCEPTUAL RELATIVITY AND SEARLE'S SCIENTIFIC NATURALISM

Before proceeding to Searle's answer to the mind-body problem, there is a final feature of Searle's thinking about fundamental ontology that bears consideration. As we have seen, Searle is committed to two, increasingly strong ontological theses: first, Searle endorses External Realism, which holds that there is a representation-independent reality. Second, Searle is committed to a substantive claim about the fine structure of this representation-independent reality: Scientific Naturalism holds that reality is basically as science describes it as being: subatomic particles in fields of force, organized into hierarchies of systems.

External Realism and Scientific Naturalism are *metaphysical* claims about how, in fact, the world is. Searle addresses a related puzzle, not about the nature of the world, but about the nature of the *concepts* we use to talk about the world.

Searle's fundamental ontology is compatible with two views about the nature of concepts. We can be "Metaphysical Realists" about our concepts. According to Hilary Putnam, Metaphysical Realism—or what Ian Hacking calls inherent structuralism[22]—holds that fundamental ontology is exhaustively and correctly described in *one* way:

What makes the metaphysical realist a *metaphysical* realist is his belief that there is somewhere, One True Theory (two theories which are true and complete descriptions of The World would be mere notational variants of each other). . . . [T]his belief in One True Theory requires a *ready-made* world—the world itself has to have a "built-in" structure since otherwise theories with different structures might correctly "copy" the world (from different perspectives) and truth would lose its Absolute (non-perspectival) character.[23]

Note that Metaphysical Realism, while principally a claim about the possibility of a conceptual scheme that exhaustively describes the world, also implies a certain minimal metaphysical commitment: that the world has a "'built-in' structure." This minimal metaphysical commitment is logically independent of both External Realism and Scientific Naturalism. Nevertheless, most who would endorse Scientific Naturalism would also subscribe to Metaphysical Realism: scientific descriptions rightly capture the contours of a "*ready-made* world." Scientific descriptions carve nature at its joints.

Metaphysical Realism is contrasted with Conceptual Relativity. Advocates of Conceptual Relativity, such as Thomas Kuhn[24] or Nelson Goodman,[25] hold that various descriptive schemes are incommensurable or inconsistent with each other. Because the world does not have a built-in structure, while some set of descriptions may still be held to be more accurate or appropriate than some other set, we should not expect to formulate a theory of everything which exhaustively characterizes the most general features of the world.

Is Searle a Metaphysical Realist?

Given that Scientific Naturalism and Metaphysical Realism are typically aligned, and that Searle strongly endorses the former, it would be easy to assume that he is also a Metaphysical Realist. However, Searle argues in favor of Conceptual Relativity. He asserts that

[a]ny system of classification or individuation of objects, any set of categories for describing the world, indeed, any system of representation at all is conventional, and to that extent arbitrary. The world divides up the way we divide it, and if we are ever inclined to think that our present way of dividing it is the right one, or is somehow inevitable, we can always imagine alternative systems of classification.[26]

To illustrate, Searle suggests that we can take, for example, a desk and arbitrarily draw a circle in chalk somewhere on its surface. Point within the circle and we can baptize this object a "klurg." Up until that moment a klurg in some sense did not exist, but we can now use the concept to make perfectly intelligible sentences—"klurgs are not as heavy as desks" or "you'll find the book on the klurg." We could, in this fashion, go on to invent an infinite number of arbitrary new vocabularies, each of which we could use to talk about the world.

How Can Conceptual Relativity Be Reconciled with Searle's Commitment to External Realism and Scientific Naturalism?

Conceptual Relativity is perfectly consistent with External Realism (ER). Searle thinks that it is a "mistake . . . to suppose that realism is committed to the theory that there is one best vocabulary for describing reality, that reality itself must determine how it should be described. But once again, ER . . . has no such implication."[27] External Realism holds *only* that the world is not ontologically dependent on our minds or representations. It is indifferent as to the question of whether or not there is a representational scheme that, moreover, exhaustively or canonically characterizes this external world.

Scientific Naturalism goes beyond the contention that there exists a representation-independent reality to claim that the scientific image captures the more basic, essential features of that reality. Can Searle's Conceptual Relativity be reconciled with his Scientific Naturalism? He never explicitly addresses this question. Most Scientific Naturalists are *not* Conceptual Relativists. It is difficult, but not impossible, to simultaneously hold that the world is essentially as science describes it as being, but also contend that scientific descriptions are nevertheless, to some extent, arbitrary. Searle might agree that science describes our ontological base while also holding that this ontological base can be brought under a variety of conceptual schemes. Searle grants that "different conceptual systems will generate different and apparently inconsistent descriptions of the same 'reality,'" but this should not drive us to a kind of antirealism about scientific entities. The possibility of an infinite number of conceptual schemes is compatible with Scientific Naturalism, so long as those schemes are logically commensurable. And Searle is explicit: against the conceptual relativism of Goodman, he contends that between two different conceptual schemes "the appearance of inconsistency is only an appearance." Likewise, Putnam agrees that we may unproblematically embrace two theories (not just one), so long as they are "mere notational variants of each other." The idea appears to be that Searle is a Conceptual Relativist, but does not go so far as to claim that the various schemes by which we talk about the world are potentially incommensurable. His is a mundane and weak Conceptual Relativity that allows for the possibility of talking about, for example, temperature in terms of either Fahrenheit or Celsius.

It must be emphasized that Searle's response to Putnam and Goodman allows for the possibility of overlapping schemes insofar as they apply to *ordinary* objects. Of course we could redescribe a desk in terms of *klurgs*. We can describe weight in terms of pounds or kilograms, thereby creating the surface appearance of inconsistency. It is arbitrary or pragmatic as to how the night sky is clustered into constellations. But it is not at all clear whether or not Searle thinks that this kind of macrolevel conceptual relativity extends to the microphysical world. Searle does write that "*any* system of representation at all is conventional, and to that extent arbitrary" (italics mine), which indicates that he favors a more global version of Conceptual Relativity. However, in 1984 Andrew Pickering infamously argued that the introduction of the concept of a quark in high-energy physics was not inevitable—that there are, at least in principle, alternative schema which would make successful predictions without making reference to anything like a quark.[28] Pickering's extreme scientific nominalism does not sound particularly Searlean. But, neither is it necessarily incompatible with his theoretical base. Searle is likely a Conceptual Relativist about certain scientific concepts (i.e., strings) but a Metaphysical Realist about others (i.e., electrons).

CHAPTER 2

CONSCIOUSNESS AND MATERIALIST THEORIES OF MIND

The Scientific Naturalist holds that the scientific image offers a comprehensive characterization of the world. What can be said of the manifest phenomena that cannot be neatly reconciled with this ontological base? This philosophical problematic reasserts itself over and over in Searle's writings: in *Speech Acts* and *The Construction of Social Reality*, Searle attempts to explain how language and other institutional facts such as money can be accommodated within a bare-bones scientific ontology. In *Rationality in Action*, Searle worries about whether the Scientific Naturalist can account for rationality and freedom. What is Searle's answer to the mind-body problem? How is conscious experience possible in a world that consists entirely of particles in fields of force?

Consciousness exhibits properties which seem anathema to the scientific image. In particular, consciousness involves, for Searle, subjective qualitative experience. The experience of pain, red, or envy each has a qualitative aspect; they have a what-it-feels-like aspect. These experiences are subjective in that they are not, unlike the objects of science, publically accessible. They have a unique, first-person point of view. Searle also focuses on another aspect of consciousness: many conscious states are intentional and so are implicated in the possibility of understanding. Brute facts, such as rocks and electrons, have neither subjective experience nor are they capable of intentionality or understanding. There are a number of other peculiar features of consciousness: it is unified, it has a sphere of focus, it operates under some mood or other, many conscious states require a Background understanding which is not conscious, and so on.

But Searle treats subjective qualitative experience as the principle point of differentiation between mind and body.

In Chapter 1, we quoted Frank Jackson, who considered two possible answers to the problem of locating consciousness (the manifest image) within our scientific world view (the scientific image). If consciousness cannot, somehow, be shown to figure *implicitly* in the more basic scientific ontology, then we must reject it as entirely illusory or *"merely* putative." According to Searle, both of these solutions represent unacceptable varieties of materialism. The first answer diminishes the mental so as to fit within the parameters of the physical. This is the strategy of the functionalists, identity theorists, and behaviorists. A second, more radical solution, adopted by eliminative materialists, dismisses the notion of the mental as unsalvageably archaic.

Searle accounts for the possibility of consciousness by pursuing a third course. He sees himself as championing the autonomy of the mental, while avoiding the extreme of mind-body dualism (where the mind is construed as too autonomous). But Searle attempts to achieve reconciliation with Scientific Naturalism, not by the attenuation or elimination of the mental so as to fall within predesignated parameters of the physical, but by *expanding* our conception of the physical so as to encompass the mental. In characterizing his own findings, Searle writes "there has been no question of 'naturalizing consciousness'; it already is completely natural."[1] Thus, consciousness remains a physical phenomenon, but Searle's physical base is found to be more expansive than that of other Scientific Naturalists.

SEARLE'S FOIL: MATERIALIST THEORIES OF MIND

So far as the mind-body problem is concerned, the motivation for materialism should be clear: if philosophical perplexity is ontological perplexity, the aim is to render compatible the manifest image with the better-understood scientific image. The easiest way to resolve ontological perplexity is to contend that the essential features of manifest phenomena are already scientific or, more radically, to cast off as merely illusory or putative the manifest phenomena. Variations of these basic approaches are represented by identity theories of mind, functionalism, and eliminative materialism.

Eliminative materialists such as Paul Feyerabend, Richard Rorty, and Paul Churchland treat our folk psychological vocabulary ("pain," "desire," "belief") as a kind of a protoscientific theory. Contending that this theory is unlikely to dovetail with a complete account of neurobiology, philosophers recommend its removal from the canons of scientific thought. But because science traces the outlines of our ontological base, this ruling is tantamount to a declaration of nonexistence. According to advocates of eliminative materialism,[2] mental predicates, like the words "phlogiston" or "vampire," simply fail to refer to anything.

Other philosophical theories of mind are variations on this theme. Where eliminative materialists deny that mental predicates have any referent, identity theorists (or physicalists) and functionalists argue that these same predicates simply refer to physical processes. Just as we discovered that the terms "morning star" and "evening star" in fact denote the same heavenly body (Venus), identity theorists[3] contend that neurophysiological predicates and mental predicates both denote states of the brain. In the way that heat is *nothing but* certain patterns of molecule excitation, pain denotes certain physical processes. The difference between eliminativists and physicalists lies, not in any substantive claim about what in fact exists (the scientific image), but in a disagreement over the status of mental predicates. Are they more like the term "unicorn," which refers to nothing whatsoever, or the terms "heat" or "blue," which refer to phenomena which happen to be fully characterizable in another, more primitive, ontological, lower-level vocabulary? The term "unicorn" is not subject to meaningful paraphrase.

If identity theorists and functionalists both redefine mental phenomena in terms of physical categories, what distinguishes them?

If both the identity theorists and functionalists would see mental attributions redescribed in terms of physical properties, they differ as to whether those physical properties are to be regarded as intrinsic or relational. There are, broadly speaking, two kinds of properties: relational and intrinsic. Relational properties, such as "taller than" or "caused by," concern the relative placement of two or more events or objects. Intrinsic or categorical properties are the attributes contained within an event or object, and hold irrespective of the placement of other events or objects.

For a type identity theorist, such as J. C. C. Smart, David Lewis, or D. M. Armstrong, a mental state just is a certain configuration or cluster of neurological objects; these are its intrinsic or categorical properties. The problem, however, is that the same configurations might manifest in importantly different ways (different behavior or even different qualitative states). Or alternatively, the same mental state might be realized on different physical bases. Thus, the functionalist, such as Hilary Putnam or Jerry Fodor, holds that it is not the intrinsic configuration that matters but the role the constellation of neurons plays in a larger system of inputs and outputs; this is to describe mental phenomena relationally against the other events in the causal web. By analogy, a type identity theorist about hearts would regard natural and artificial hearts as distinct because they are composed of different materials. A functionalist about hearts would regard them as more or less equivalent, because both organs play the same causal role in the body.

Finally, token identity theorists concede, against the type identity theorist, that it is unlikely that the same mental event will always be instantiated on the same physical base. But they are anxious about letting functional, relational attributions be the final word in the individuation of mental states. This may be because some philosophers, such as W. V. O. Quine, have recommended that such relational predicates are shorthand for intrinsic, categorical descriptions: to describe something as soluble is shorthand for a (perhaps as-of-yet unknown) description in terms of the intrinsic structure of that thing. This is to say that certain considerations should move us to reduce functionalism to an identity theory. Of course, the token identity solution creates its own difficulties: there appear to be no criteria by which to identify two physical states as the same kind of thing—the same mental state.

In conclusion, the materialists adopt two basic strategies in reconciling the mental with the scientific image. The eliminative materialist claims that the mental does not denote anything. Other theorists do not eliminate mental terminology but contend that the important features of the mental are anyway physical. Within the latter camp, there are a number of different criteria by which these theorists come to individuate mental events.

SEARLE'S CRITIQUES OF MATERIALIST THEORIES OF MIND

Physical Systems Have No Phenomenology

Eliminative materialism, identity theories, and functionalism each have problems associated with their specific articulation of a materialist theory of mind. Searle's criticisms, however, attack the very idea of a materialist theory of mind. Eliminative materialism, identity theories, and functionalism are each expressions of a pattern that Searle thinks is wrongheaded; he identifies this tendency as

> a recurring tension between the urge to give an account of reality that leaves out any reference to the special features of the mental, such as consciousness and subjectivity, and at the same time account for our "intuitions" about the mind.[4]

In particular Searle claims that materialist theories, trying to naturalize the mind, end up eviscerating the vital, qualitative, what-it-feels-like aspect of consciousness. Materialists treat the subjective aspect as incidental, whereas Searle contends that anything that is not first personal is not a candidate for consciousness. Searle shares the project—the task is to "locate consciousness within our overall 'scientific' conception of the world"[5]—but worries that the materialist's solution is cheap insofar as it achieves reconciliation through varieties of elimination.

Searle's principle worry is that materialist conceptions of mind leave out the first-person, what-it-feels-like subjectivity that is essential to one's being conscious. Searle sometimes paraphrases this subjectivity in terms of awareness or sensations. Other philosophers speak of this subjective quality in terms of phenomenology or qualia. Pain, for example, may have a neurophysiological component but there is an essential *feeling*, over and above the brain events, that constitutes my being in pain. All of these descriptors drive at the experiential quality that Searle takes to be indicative of consciousness.

All varieties of materialism fail precisely because, in attempting to account for the mental in third-person terms (in terms which render the mind accessible to the sciences) they end up eliminating this essential qualitative aspect.

To demonstrate this, Searle rehearses and provides a number of arguments meant to remind us that subjectivity is logically distinct from, and so irreducible to, the third-person base.

Classic arguments to this effect are offered by Thomas Nagel, Frank Jackson, and Saul Kripke. In Nagel's "What is it Like to be a Bat?"[6] he argues that we can only attribute mental properties to an organism (such as a bat) if and only if there is a particular *way* in which the organism can be said to experience the world. We do not know what it is like to perceive the world by way of a kind of sonar. Whatever this experience may be, it cannot be understood by even a complete understanding of the bat's neurophysiology. Similarly, Jackson[7] has us imagine a brilliant neuroscientist—Mary—who is raised in conditions such that she has never seen color. The room in which she lives and studies is black and white, as is the television by which she accesses the world. She has, furthermore, a perfect understanding of the processes which underlie our seeing colors. In this case, Mary still does not know something about what it is to see red. Both arguments show that the first-person qualitative experience is not reducible to a third-person quantitative understanding of the neurobiology on which the bat's and Mary's experience depends.

While Searle endorses Nagel's and Jackson's arguments for the autonomy of consciousness, he also presents two of his own. In the Silicon Brains thought experiment,[8] Searle has the reader imagine that they are going blind: after a number of treatments, the subject resorts to planting silicon chips in the visual cortex, which somehow restores vision. Unfortunately, other parts of the brain begin to atrophy and are likewise replaced by silicon chips. This continues to happen until the entire nervous system is replaced with silicon surrogates. While we don't know what would actually happen, Searle sees three possibilities. First, the transplantation process would have little effect on either the subject's behavior or conscious mental life. Second, it is possible that while the subject's behavior continues unabated, consciousness subsides with every new transplant until it disappears, as if in a deep sleep. Finally, the inverse is possible, so that while consciousness is retained, the subject gradually becomes unable to exert control over the body, falling into paralysis.

The force of this thought experiment is as follows: without having to say which of these three possibilities would, in fact, happen, by merely agreeing that these represent genuine alternatives we are already agreeing that the concepts of *consciousness* and *behavior* are logically distinct. If notions of mind and body were interdefined, as the materialist would have it, it would make no more sense to contend that a person could behave without being conscious (possibility 3), than claim to be a bachelor without being male. But because consciousness is conceptually isolated from behavior, this is evidence for the stronger claim that consciousness is not conceptually interdefined with the physical.

Note that this argument appears puzzling given Searle's positive view of consciousness. As we will see, Searle grants that consciousness is both caused by, and a feature of, the underlying neurophysiology.

If it is not so caused, it does not qualify as consciousness, as changes in consciousness must be underlain by changes in the brain. But given that consciousness is thus defined in terms of its physical causes, consciousness does *not* appear to be conceptually isolated from the physical, broadly construed to include the neural happenings. The Silicon Brains thought experiment argues that behavior is conceptually distinct from consciousness, but elsewhere Searle seems to deny that consciousness can be isolated from neurological events or behavior.

In a second thought experiment called "Conscious Robots,"[9] Searle has us imagine a robot that has subjective experience. Perhaps the robot, due to a burdensome workload, experiences a great deal of misery. In response, its makers turn off its ability to be conscious. This procedure has no effect on its behavior. This shows, like the Silicon Brains experiment, that our concept of consciousness is not conceptually tied to our concept of behavior. But materialists in general, and functionalists in particular, wish to see the notion of consciousness collapse into the scientific image, which includes physical behavior.

Physical Systems Have No Intentional Understanding

The Chinese Room argument is Searle's most famous attack on a materialist theory of mind called Strong Artificial Intelligence ("Strong AI"). Here, an essentially functionalist account of mind is coupled with a vivid metaphor, so that the brain is compared to a computer, whereas the mind would be a computer program. This analogy provides the basis for a fecund research program spearheaded by departments of cognitive science. Because a computer can be realized on any number of physical platforms, what distinguishes computers from noncomputers and so by analogy mental processes from nonmental processes, is some formal configuration of inputs and outputs.

The Chinese Room argument concludes that a formally described system cannot, in itself, give rise to *intentional understanding*. Like the Silicon Brains and Conscious Robots arguments, the Chinese Room argues that something essential is left out when mental phenomena are construed exclusively in terms of their physical base. But where the first two thought experiments claim that the materialist (including the functionalist) disregards the *subjective experience* essential to consciousness, the Chinese Room argument contends that the functionalist-cum-strong-AI-theorist wrongly construes the nature of *intentional understanding*.

What is intentional understanding and what is its relation to the subjective experience, the target of the Silicon Brains and Conscious Robots arguments?

Some mental states are *intentional*, here defined technically as mental states that represent or are about things. The term captures the way in which our thoughts, attitudes, beliefs, and desires are *directed*, in various ways, toward the world. Intentional beliefs concern the way that the world is, and our desires concern how we would like things to be. The concept of intentionality is a centerpiece of Searle's philosophy of mind.

The Chinese Room argument targets the representationalist account of intentional understanding. Searle's own summary of the Chinese Room argument is as follows:

> Imagine a native English speaker who knows no Chinese locked in a room full of boxes of Chinese symbols (a database) together with a book of instructions for manipulating the symbols (the program). Imagine that people outside the room send in other Chinese symbols which, unknown to the person in the room, are questions in Chinese (the input). And imagine that by following the instructions in the program the man in the room is able to pass out Chinese symbols which are correct answers to the questions (the output). The program enables the person in the room to pass the Turing Test for understanding Chinese but he does not understand a word of Chinese.[10]

According to the functionalist, mental states are defined relationally in terms of their causes (inputs) and effects (outputs). The Chinese Room experiment is also intended to capture certain features of the computationalist flavor of functionalism, wherein the mind is compared to a program. Programs transform symbols according to certain rules. The book of instructions for symbol manipulation, to which the English speaker has access, is the program. If the Chinese Room is given a series of questions, it is able to correctly answer those questions—so that, functionally speaking, its behavior mirrors a well-informed, native Chinese speaker. The Turing Test, formulated by Alan Turing in 1950,[11] proposes a criterion by which a machine can be said to be intelligent or capable of understanding. If I am interacting with both a machine and human (over a text-only channel, such as internet messaging or email), and I cannot reliably distinguish which is which, the machine will have passed the Turing test. Searle's point is that even if the Chinese Room passes the Turing test, we would not say that the man inside the room *understands* what he, or the Chinese Room, is saying. Thus, the Turing test's benchmark for intelligence does not permit us to say, of the machine, that it understands. In particular, the English speaker's symbol manipulation is blind, lacking the intentional aboutness essential to understanding.

The point is sometimes put as follows: syntactical manipulation is not sufficient for semantics. Logic concerns the articulation of procedures by which to draw reliable inferences from a set of propositions. These syntactical rules hold irrespective of the particular semantic content contained in these propositions, so that logical connections still hold if we replace a sentence's nouns and adjectives with dummy letters. Using this model, the computationalist wishes to find a set of rules or conditional procedures which exhaust the scope of mental activity. If mental states are *about* something, and so have specific semantic content, computationalism attempts to capture this intentionality through the multiplication of underlying syntactical rules and procedures. To understand something *just is* to exhibit the right response given certain stimuli. But the Chinese Room is designed to demonstrate that semantics—intentional understanding—can never be derived from a syntax or set of procedures. Part of the thought experiment's effectiveness stems from its not placing any limitations on the complexity of the rule book; no amplification of rules can, by itself, amount to the symbol manipulator's understanding of the questions asked or the answers given.

The Chinese Room argument is logically independent of Searle's Silicon Brains argument, which claims that mental phenomena have an essential qualitative aspect. It shows that intentional representation cannot be reduced to formally defined relations. The dummy symbols manipulated in the Chinese Room do not mean anything to the manipulator. In arguing this, Searle is arguing that intentional understanding cannot be reduced to functional, physicalist systems.

While he endorses Scientific Naturalism, he resists the attempt to construe the mental in terms which are reduced without remainder to a scientific-ontological base. The Silicon Brains and Conscious

Robots arguments show that there is a gap between subjective qualitative experience and that scientific base. The Chinese Room argument shows that there is a gap between intentional understanding (representation) and that same base. As we will see, the former arguments are in many ways more important, as, on Searle's view, all intentional understanding depends on the possibility of subjective-qualitative experience.

Consciousness and Intentional Understanding

Searle has argued that qualitative experience and intentional understanding are irreducible to the scientific image. What is the relationship between these two essentially irreducible features of mind?

Broadly speaking, there are two views of mental representation.[12] The phenomenalists, including Searle, understand mental representation along the lines of a picture, so that mental representation always has a qualitative aspect. The representationalists understand mental representation in terms of information processing. Information about things must be causally linked to that thing, but does not need to have an additional qualitative aspect. For example, there is a crude sense in which a thermostat understands or is responsive to the ambient temperature for the representationalist. However, Searle as well as other phenomenalists assert that the what-it-feels-like quality indicative of subjectivity is a *precondition* for intentional understanding.

While Searle is better known for the Chinese Room argument, in many ways the conclusion of the Silicon Brains or Conscious Robots arguments are more salient. Mind is conscious in that it has an essential subjective and qualitative aspect. *Some* of these conscious states—intentional states—may also be said to exhibit intentional understanding. Thus while understanding requires consciousness, the inverse is not true: some nonintentional states, such as some kinds of pain or pleasures, are merely qualitative. Intentional states also have an object. While some mental states are also intentional, it is clear that the qualitative what-it-feels like aspect is the defining feature of mind.

This conceptual hierarchy is underscored in an argument called the Connection Principle,[13] which elucidates the relationship between the conscious and the unconscious. Consciousness is necessarily qualitative. Unconscious states are not: when sleeping, the sweeping of my hand might suggest that I *unconsciously* recognize a mosquito on my face, but I am not experiencing the tickle of insect legs or the sound of its wings. My behavior might suggest that I have certain beliefs that are not otherwise consciously available to me. What distinguishes an unconscious desire to swat a mosquito from a thermostat's propensity to turn on the heater, if neither has a qualitative, subjective component? That is, unconscious mental states are contrasted with two kinds of events: neither are they *conscious* mental states, nor are they merely physical, blind states or events. They are not conscious because they lack the subjective qualitative aspect, but why not, as Nietzsche does,[14] regard them as among the blind, nonmental phenomena described by science?

According to Searle, unconscious intentional states are differentiated from blind causal happenings insofar as they are *potentially* conscious. There is no possibility of a thermostat's being aware of a desire to turn on the heat in the way that I could be aware of a desire to swat a mosquito, and so such intentionalistic attributions could only be metaphorical. The point is, unconscious mental states are doubly dispositional: they tend, like the thermostat, to bring about certain behavior and, unlike the thermostat, they must be also able to potentially manifest certain conscious states.

Recall that for the representationalist, the first-person subjective or phenomenal experience is just one kind of representational, intentional content; the aim is to reduce consciousness to the more fundamental ability to represent the world. Accordingly, a thought or perception refers to, for example, a desk because it was caused by desks; following this causal-information theory, qualitative mental imagery is not necessary to account for an intentional state's ability to be *about* things.[15] Thermostats represent temperature. But according to the connection principle, the representationalist has it exactly backwards. The qualitative aspect of consciousness is a precondition for understanding, insofar as intentional representation must be at least potentially conscious. According to Searle, if the brain state is not at least potentially conscious or phenomenal, it is disqualified from being a kind of representational, intentional state. Thus the connection principle excludes a great deal of what the functionalist or representationalist might count as an intentional mental state. Thermostats do not represent the temperature because they are not even potentially conscious. If understanding implies the possibility of a subjective qualitative experience, this explains why Searle's, Nagel's, and Jackson's arguments for the irreducibility of subjective experience is more central to the former's conception of mind than is the Chinese Room argument.

Both phenomenalists and representationalists agree that intentionality is a basic property of the mind; but Searle's connection principle aims to show that the subjective, phenomenal properties of consciousness are *more* basic than the intentional ones, insofar as the latter require at least the possibility of the former. This conviction is reflected in Searle's dividing mental processes into intentional and nonintentional, strictly phenomenal states. In that way, the connection principle is less an attempt to elucidate the idea of the unconscious and more an argument for a phenomenalist theory of mind and mental representation.

SEARLE'S ANSWER TO THE MIND-BODY PROBLEM: BIOLOGICAL NATURALISM

Much of *The Rediscovery of the Mind* is dedicated to a rejection of the materialist theories of mind. Searle shares with the materialist a scientific metaphysics, wherein the fundamental ingredients of the universe are roughly as physics describes them as being. But where materialists attempt to *reduce* higher-level mental properties, such as phenomenology and understanding, to the lower-level theoretical base, Searle wishes only to *reconcile* the former with the latter. Indeed, he regards these higher-level phenomena as importantly autonomous:

> [O]ne can accept the obvious facts of physics—that the world consists entirely of physical particles in fields of force—without denying that among the physical features of the world are biological phenomena such as inner qualitative states of consciousness and intrinsic intentionality.[16]

The mind-body problem concerns how the mind can be reconciled with the body in such a way that maintains the mind's integrity without bowing to ontological dualism, which totalizes the separation. Searle then hopes to chart a course between two extremes. According to dualism, mental phenomena are regarded as so unlike physical phenomena as to be ontologically distinct. Dualism is correct in that it captures the sense in which mental phenomena are autonomous, but overstates the insight by making such states irreconcilable with the theoretical base. Dualism is incompatible with Searle's commitment to Scientific Naturalism.

In short, Searle achieves the desired reconciliation by *expanding his ontological base to include consciousness,* rather than collapsing the mental so as to accord with an apriori conception of that ontological base. It is not, then, that the mental stands in need of naturalizing; Searle argues that the notion of the natural, rather, is already inclusive enough to encompass consciousness.

How is consciousness construed as natural? A reader could be forgiven for thinking that Searle is being temerarious when he opens the *Rediscovery of the Mind* with an answer to that question.

> The famous mind-body problem, the source of so much controversy over the past two millennia, has a simple solution. This solution has been available to any educated person since serious work began on the brain nearly a century ago, and, in a sense, we all know it to be true. Here it is: Mental phenomena are caused by neurophysiological processes in the brain and are themselves features of the brain.[17]

Brain processes fall unproblematically within the scope of the scientific image. Because consciousness is, first, caused by those natural processes and, second, a feature of those processes, Searle thinks that consciousness should not be any more troubling to the naturalist than is the underlying neurobiology.

Along these lines, Searle recommends that consciousness stands to the brain as digestion stands to the movements of the stomach, boiling stands to the rapid movements of the underlying particles, or phenotypes stand to genotypes. More generally put, Searle asserts that in addition to standard, temporal, left-right, Humean causation (low pressure causes the storm to move), there is also a down-up causation, where macroproperties are explained by appeal to the behavior of microproperties. Macroeconomic fluctuations, such as increased inflation, are a function of billions of microtransactions taking place. A full accounting of consumer behavior already fully explains the inflation. According to Searle, then, there is no more a mind-body problem than there is a macro-micro economics problem. They are different levels of description of the same set of phenomena.

Moreover, the standard left-right causation involves a relation between two distinct objects or events—the low-pressure zone and the movement of the storm. Thus you can, at least in principle, have a low-pressure zone without storm movement, or visa versa. But the relata involved in up-down causation are not so distinct. Inflation is concomitant with certain patterns of microeconomic transactions, and certain patterns of microeconomic transactions can be redescribed as inflation.

Apart from these suggestive examples, Searle gives readers relatively little help in disentangling the significance of his view. One difficulty is that physicalists might actually agree that the mental is a biological, higher-order feature of the brain. And just as macroeconomic movements can be redescribed, without remainder, in terms of microlevel transactions, the physicalists might contend that mental concepts can be described, without remainder, in terms of the working of the microlevel neural processes. Searle's analogies seem compatible with materialist agendas.[18] This conception of the mind, where it is caused by and is a feature of the brain, does not, in itself, render the mental sufficiently autonomous.

But Searle is careful to maintain that the mental—the domain of qualitative experience and understanding—is autonomous and has no counterpart on the microlevel; any redescription of these macrolevel features amounts to a kind of evisceration, in a way that isn't the case with the economic analogy. A microlevel articulation of inflation is, to be sure, more complicated, but would nevertheless preserve the entirety of the macrolevel patterns. We could, similarly, describe the workings of a car engine at two levels of description: at the level of molecules or at the level of pistons and cylinders. But the lower-level description seems only to account for the higher-level motion with a kind of increased resolution or precision; nothing is lost. But unless the atomic, molecular, and/or neural systems which give rise to consciousness are, in some way, already conscious, then the analogy breaks down: the materialist might agree that mental events are higher-order descriptions according to Searle's formula, but not at all be inclined to further grant that the mental has irreducible, qualitative features. Indeed, Searle's digestion and economic metaphors seem to speak against this possibility.

In the end, there is a gap between Searle's claim that mental states are both caused by, and a feature of, underlying neurobiological states and the stronger suggestion that mental states are irreducibly qualitative or subjective. Searle, along with Jackson and Nagel, has offered powerful arguments in favor of the view that consciousness cannot be completely redescribed in microphysical terms; but Searle's claim that mental states are caused by and a feature of the neurophysiology are not among these arguments.[19]

But if, according to the Silicon Brains argument, subjective qualitative first-personal experience cannot be reduced to microlevel properties, how, then, is Searle going to reconcile these macrolevel features with the ontological base? Searle appears to achieve reconciliation between the scientific image and manifest image by simply stretching the domain of the former to include the latter:

> The problem we face with the terminology is that the terms have traditionally been defined so as to be mutually exclusive. "Mental" is defined as qualitative, subjective, first personal, and therefore immaterial. "Physical" is defined as quantitative, objective, third personal, and therefore material. I am suggesting that these definitions are inadequate to capture the fact that the world works in such a way that some biological processes are qualitative, subjective, and first personal. If we are going to keep this terminology at all, we need an expanded notion of the physical to allow for its intrinsic, subjective mental component.[20]

Searle grants that there is an important difference between what has been regarded as the physical and the mental. Physical features are ontologically objective, in that they are accessible to a variety of observers. Mental features are, by contrast, ontologically subjective in that any given set of experiences are only accessible to a single observer. Searle sees no reason to identify the extension of the term "natural" with only those phenomena which happen to be third-person accessible (ontologically objective). Epistemic points—modes of accessibility—should have little to do with determinations of basic ontology. The fact that certain events happen to be accessible only to an individual person need not impugn on their reality. The problem with the standard mind-body distinction is that it pegs, too tightly, questions of ontology to an unrelated epistemic question concerning modes of accessibility.

Searle's fundamental ontology *includes* subjective mental states. This inclusion gives Searle the very means to articulate a distinction between ontologically objective and ontologically subjective phenomena; these are *both* a part of our basic ontology. While both are "physical" in Searle's extended notion of the word, only the former is "physical" in the traditional sense of the word—as denoting third-person accessible phenomena such as electrons and mountains.

Searle calls the view that expands the notion of the physical to include ontologically subjective mental states "Biological Naturalism," which is a kind of Scientific Naturalism. Other versions of Scientific Naturalism about the mind, such as eliminative materialism, functionalism, or identity theories, truncate the concept of mind so as to fit within a predetermined, narrow, third-person accessible conception of the physical.

I will conclude with a brief discussion of the significance of this strategy, as it relates to Searle's own claim that he is a Scientific Naturalist. The aim is to offer a more general characterization of the move made in extending the notion of the physical so as to include consciousness.

Recall the anomalous limestone blocks found on the pyramids at Giza. Among other peculiar features, the blocks contain higher amounts of silicon than is found in other sources of limestone. A working explanation for these anomalies is that the blocks were cast rather than cut; silicon serves as a binding agent. Critics of this study have pointed out that silicon is a common geologic element, so the fact that it is found in the limestones does not merit explanation. What has happened here?

Briefly, Bas van Fraassen has suggested that in order for a why-question to arise it must satisfy a number of conditions. One of these is that the object under investigation must have a contrast-class—a set of expectations which renders the explanandum anomalous or unexpected.[21] For the researchers, the contrast-class is found in the claim that silicon is not typically found in limestone. Thus, the silicon becomes an object of explanation: why do *these* limestone blocks have silicon in them? And its presence is explained by the fact that the blocks were not quarried, but cast using silicon as a binding agent. So far, so good. However, if critics contend that silicon is in fact ubiquitous, that is tantamount to claiming that the why-question has no contrast-class and, thus, *does not arise*. The worry here is not that the explanation (the blocks were cast) is *bad*; this is the much stronger claim that there is simply nothing to explain in the first place. The presence of silicon in limestone was not unexpected, in that it does not violate any known chemical and geological theories. It is indeed anticipated by these theories, and so is not a proper object of explanation.

Against the dualist and materialist, Searle can be observed as making an analogous move. Both the dualist and materialist regard subjective, qualitative states as anomalous against expectations embodied in the scientific image (the contrast-class): how can a natural world, which consists of blind particles in fields of force, give rise to qualitative, subjective consciousness? While materialism and dualism present competing explanatory strategies, the very fact that they are attempting to explain consciousness already constitutes a tacit endorsement of the question. This is comparable to the researcher's attempt to explain the fact that certain blocks contain appreciable amounts of silicon. What Searle does, against both the materialist and dualist, is *reject the question*. The natural world *already* contains consciousness, so that there is no contrast-class against which the materialist's or dualist's question gains traction. Just as we do not have to explain the presence of silicon if its presence is already accounted for by our geological theories, we are not obliged to explain the presence of consciousness if it is already part of the natural world. Consciousness does not conflict with Searle's version of Scientific Naturalism, but rather helps constitute it. Materialism and dualism are mutually exclusive categories only against a question that Searle does not accept:

When confronted with an intractable question such as is presented by a clash of convincing default positions, don't accept the question lying down. Get up and go behind the question to see what assumptions lie behind the alternatives the question presents. In this case, we did not answer the question in terms of the alternatives presented to us but we *overcame* the question. The question was, is dualism or materialism the correct analysis of the mental? The answer is: as traditionally conceived, neither; as revised, both. Hence it is best to reject the vocabulary of "dualism" and "materialism" altogether and start over.[22]

CHAPTER 3

INTENTIONAL MENTAL STATES

Searle's Biological Naturalism attempts to reconcile the mental with the physical while avoiding the excesses of both materialism and dualism. He distinguishes the mental from the physical insofar as the former has an irreducible experiential, subjective component. Materialist theories of mind miss the vital fact that mental states have a what-it-feels-like quality which is not accessible to any outside observer. Pain is an actual feature of the world, even if the experience is not intersubjectively available.

Searle further divides the mental into intentional and nonintentional phenomena. While both must be potentially conscious, intentional mental states are *about* things in a way that nonintentional states are not. Nonintentional states, such as pain, are not about anything at all: they count as mental states because they have the requisite phenomenology, but pain does not, or need not, represent anything outside of itself.

Searle's distinction between intentional and nonintentional mental states is intuitive but not uncontroversial. Contra Searle, representationalists see the aboutness characteristic of intentional states as the *defining* mark of the mental. Some of these theorists might then go on to subdivide the mental according to whether it happens also to be conscious, so inverting Searle's prioritization. All mental states, including pain, which is perhaps about the state of one's body, are intentional. Searle is a phenomenalist, in that he regards the subjective, qualitative aspect to be more fundamental to the concept of the mental. Nevertheless, he agrees with the representationalist that many mental states are also about things. He uses the word "intentionality" to denote this important subset of mental states, which represent or have a characteristic aboutness.

In this chapter we review Searle's fine-grained account of the aboutness characteristic of intentional states. How, and, in what ways, are our intentional states able to represent the world?

AN IMPERFECT ANALOGY: INTENTIONAL CONTENT AS A MODEL

How can something be *about* or *represent* some other thing? We can get some insight into the peculiarities of Searle's view by looking at scientific models, which are representations of some target system. Copernicus' heliocentric model of the universe locates the sun, rather than the earth, at the center of the universe. Intuitively, Copernicus' model represents the universe by somehow *resembling* it.

To be clear, the analogy between the intentional states and models, pictures, or sentences breaks down quickly.[1] Searle is quick—perhaps too quick—to disavow the connection:

> When I say, for example, that a belief is a representation I am most emphatically not saying that a belief is a kind of picture, nor am I endorsing the *Tractatus* account of meaning, nor am I saying that a belief re-presents something that has been presented before, nor am I saying that a belief has a meaning. . . .[2]

Indeed, Searle is going to explain a model's or picture's capacity to represent by appeal to the mind's capacity to represent. Still, in other places, Searle emphasizes the analogy between mental representation and picturing or modeling; as we will see, both intentionality and models represent the world as being a certain way, by way of what Searle calls *conditions of satisfaction*. Both mental representation and models can get the world wrong or right, under varying degrees of idealization. The difference is that pictures get their capacity to represent, not just by virtue of their physically mirroring the world, but derivatively, by way of our innate capacity for mental representation.[3] While Searle is quite right to deny that intentional states are like little portraits in the mind,[4] the comparison is nevertheless helpful in drawing out three features of Searle's account of intentionality.

First, and most importantly, the analogy between models and intentional states nicely illustrates the sense in which, for Searle, mental states are fundamentally *counterfactual*.

Both modeling and representation entail the very human ability to see the world or universe as other than it might in fact be. I can imagine a world in which I own a red car rather than a grey car. I can imagine a world in which, as of 2007, George W. Bush was not president. I can imagine a world which contains no people in it. I can also imagine (or represent) the world correctly, as it is.

A model of the universe is not the universe; it is a kind of portrayal, description, or mirror image of the universe. Because an intentional state both reflects, and is distinguishable from, its object, it can be *otherwise*. Mental representations and models represent a possible universe that stands in various relations with the actual universe: these relations allow us to speak of both intentional states and models in terms of their being accurate, right, wrong, misleading, vague, and so on.

So, both models and mental representations depict a possible world (W_p).[5] Furthermore, this represented, possible universe might either be identical with the actual world (W_a), or else diverge from the actual world.[6] In the latter case, W_p and W_a would not be isomorphic. In a simple example, I can represent a possible world in which my closet is full (W_p), when in fact in the actual world it is empty (W_a). In this case the represented content diverges from how the world in fact is: $W_p \neq W_a$.

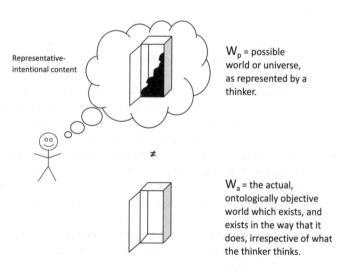

Representative-intentional content

W_p = possible world or universe, as represented by a thinker.

$\neq$

W_a = the actual, ontologically objective world which exists, and exists in the way that it does, irrespective of what the thinker thinks.

The represented content targets an intentional state's *conditions of satisfaction*. Unfortunately Searle uses the phrase in two, overlapping ways, causing considerable trouble for his interpreters. Getting clearer on his notion of conditions of satisfaction requires that we first understand his notion of *psychological mode*, in the next section.

There is a second point of analogy between intentional states and models. Insofar as a represented possible world is not identical to the actual world, the possible can be distinguished from the actual world in two ways: it can be accurate but incomplete (idealized) or it can be simply inaccurate.

Copernicus' model is more similar to the universe than is Ptolemy's. Moreover, these represented worlds do not just bear a relationship of similarity to the actual world, but are partial or incomplete.[7] There are two importantly different senses in which Copernicus' heliocentric model is not about *our* universe, but about a universe which is somewhat similar to our own. First, the model is idealized or *globally* inaccurate: it is about a universe which is much simpler than the actual universe. The model is partial or incomplete. It doesn't purport to account for, for example, the movement of comets or the behavior of the people on one of the planets. Planets and their motion are treated within a crystalline, geometric framework. So in some sense the model is about a different, simplified universe, as compared to our own. Likewise, the content of intentional states, like that of scientific models, represents our universe under a certain aspect. Even when W_p is in accordance with W_a, it remains globally inaccurate.

The second sense in which the content of an intentional state may not be about *our* universe, but some possible universe, is simply that it may *wrongly* represent our own world. A model or intentional state may inaccurately represent our world in a way that is stronger than being an oversimplification or idealization. That is, a model or content may be *locally* inaccurate if it misrepresents the features that it is trying to represent. If we confine our attention to the subset of features a representation purports to be about—such as if we ignore the fact that humans are living on earth and focus only on relevant features such as planetary size, position, and motion—a representation may still fail to fit the world. Copernicus' model, for example, postulates that the planets revolve around the sun in perfect circles when in fact they trace ellipses. The representation is locally inaccurate because it fails to rightly depict even that aspect of the world that it concerns—planetary motion. Another way of putting this is that Copernicus' model represents the motion of planets in a possible (W_p), but not an actual (W_a), universe.

The difference between a representation's being globally and locally inaccurate amounts to the claim that there are different ways in which there can be a gap between intentional content and the actual world. In saying that we can imagine the world to be other than it is, Searle is drawing our attention to our ability to depict the world in *locally* inaccurate ways. The fact that our representations are also globally inaccurate is unremarkable and is tantamount to the view that we can only represent certain aspects of the world at a time. If a belief is only idealized or globally inaccurate, that does not necessarily call for revision; only if a belief is locally inaccurate would it ordinarily be said to be *false*.

There is a third and final way in which an intentional state might be compared to a model. If a model represents an object, it doesn't necessarily do so simply by virtue of its being causally connected with that object. While it is undeniable that Copernicus' model was the result of empirical observations, and so caused by the universe, this causal connection was not, at least in 1610, robust enough to distinguish this model from Ptolemy's terra-centric or Tycho's hybrid model. Assuming that each of these models could account for, and were formulated in response to the facts, these are nevertheless *different* models—something for which the causalist cannot account. Note that this third provision targets representationalist accounts of mental representation, which require a causal connection between object and belief.

PSYCHOLOGICAL MODES

Given the analogy between intentional states and scientific modeling, we are now in a position to present the entirety of Searle's theory of intentionality.

Intentional states represent their objects. The part of the intentional state that represents these objects is called its *representative content*. The representative content is analogous to a model. The content represents a possible world—its conditions of satisfaction—which may or may not correspond to the actual world.

One other ingredient is needed to formulate the bare bones of Searle's account of intentionality—what Searle calls the *psychological mode*.

Generally speaking, the psychological mode of an intentional state specifies the manner in which one *uses* the representative content. In speech, I can do a number of things with a given representative content: I can assert something, I can express a desire, or I can make a promise. I can say: "I want to wash the car," or "I promise to wash the car," or, "The car is washed." In doing so, I have brought the same content (washed car) under different modes or uses. Similarly, Searle is impressed by the fact that I can have a number of different intentional states which nevertheless can have a shared content— I can think: *The car is washed*, or *I wish the car were washed*, or *I will wash the car*. In each case I am treating the same representative content in a variety of different ways.

With the notion of *direction of fit* Searle subdivides the various kinds of psychological modes into a manageable pair of classes. Psychological modes exhibit either a mind-to-world (downward) or a world-to-mind (upward) direction of fit.

When the representative content represents a possible world which diverges from the actual world (so that the content is locally inaccurate), the divergence only tells us that there is a gap or mis-fit which needs to be rectified. The direction of fit tells us *how* the gap between the represented possible world and the actual world ought to be closed. If my intentional content represents a possible world wherein my closet is full, and the actual world is such that it isn't, the gap between the represented conditions of satisfaction and the actual state of my closet can be closed by either (1) changing the representative content and so changing the conditions of satisfaction or (2) by filling my closet so as to come into line with the original represented content. In either case, the represented possible world is brought into alignment with the actual world.

If there is a discrepancy between the represented possible world and the actual world, when would I close that gap by *changing the intentional content*? I change the intentional content when my aim is to accurately represent the world so that the content functions in the service of a *belief*. I have a false belief about the state of my closet (it represents a non-actual, possible world in which my closet is full) and so change it to represent the world as it actually is. Beliefs have what

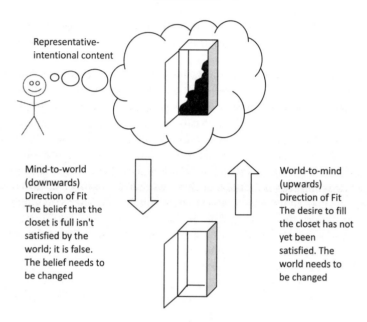

Representative-
intentional content

Mind-to-world
(downwards)
Direction of Fit
The belief that the
closet is full isn't
satisfied by the
world; it is false.
The belief needs to
be changed

World-to-mind
(upwards)
Direction of Fit
The desire to fill
the closet has not
yet been
satisfied. The
world needs to
be changed

Searle calls a mind-to-world or downward direction of fit: beliefs ought to fit the world.

Where belief is the paradigm case of a psychological mode that stands in a mind-to-world direction of fit, there are other modes that likewise fall under this category. For example, I might be convinced, predict, postulate, suspect, worry, conclude, or fear that some content stands in a true or false relationship to the world.

If the same representative content is brought under a different psychological mode (than those which have a mind-to-world direction of fit, such as belief), I can close the gap by *changing the world* (rather than by changing the content). If the content functions in the service of the psychological mode, a *desire* to have a full closet, then I can make the possible world actual by filling my closet. Desires have a world-to-mind, upward direction of fit: the world should be made to match the mind's content. Desire is the paradigm case of a psychological mode with a world-to-mind direction of fit. I might also wish, hope, will, or intend (in the narrower sense of the word) that the world be changed in a certain way.

Psychological mode, and the associated notion of direction of fit, has a correlate in modeling: models are typically more akin to beliefs than desires, in that they attempt to portray the world as it is and not as we might like it to be. However, some models can serve as normative ideals, and so have a world-to-mind direction of fit—as when an economic libertarian attempts to push policies to bring the actual market closer to the ideal of a free market.[8]

An intentional state's direction of fit, then, captures the way in which all intentional states are inherently *normative*: intentional thought implies, at its base, the possibility of getting it wrong—or, more generally, misrepresenting how the world actually is. Both a false belief and a desire require that we can represent the world counterfactually, as other than it is. In case of a mis-fit, we are then impelled to rectify the divergence. Searle writes that, "Intuitively we might say the idea of direction of fit is that of responsibility for fitting."[9] This comes out somewhat more clearly when Searle writes:

> For any Intentional state with a direction of fit, a being that has that state must be able to distinguish the satisfaction from the frustration of that state. This follows from the fact that an Intentional state is a representation of the conditions of its satisfaction. This does not mean that such beings will always or even most of the time get it right, that they won't make mistakes; rather, it means that they must have the capacity for recognizing what it would be to get it right.[10]

The representative content creates conditions for the possibility of a mis-fit between mind and world. But the psychological mode governs how we *ought* to proceed in rectifying that mis-fit if, on the one hand, the content is in the service of a belief, we need to change the content (change the conditions of satisfaction). If, on the other hand, the content is in the service of a desire, we satisfy it by changing the world.

We are now in a position to better understand Searle's notion of *conditions of satisfaction*. The problem is that sometimes Searle uses the phrase, so far as beliefs are concerned, to flag the possible world as represented by the thinker (W_p) and sometimes uses the phrase to flag the actual world (W_a). Searle's use of the phrase is not so much incoherent as it is muddled. However, the sense in which he uses the phrase is almost always transparent in context.

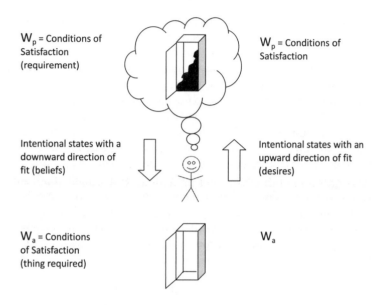

W$_p$ = Conditions of Satisfaction (requirement)

W$_p$ = Conditions of Satisfaction

Intentional states with a downward direction of fit (beliefs)

Intentional states with an upward direction of fit (desires)

W$_a$ = Conditions of Satisfaction (thing required)

W$_a$

Confining his attention to beliefs, Searle attempts to rectify the ambiguity as follows:

> The expression "conditions of satisfaction" has the usual process-product ambiguity as between the *requirement* and the *thing required.* So, for example, if I believe that it is raining then the conditions of satisfaction of my belief are that it should be the case *that it is raining* (requirement). That is what my belief requires in order that it be a true belief. And if my belief actually is a true belief then there will be a certain condition in the world, namely the condition *that it is raining* (thing required), which is the condition of the satisfaction of my belief, i.e., the condition in the world which actually satisfies my belief.[11]

I have a belief, with a downward direction of fit, that the closet is full (W$_p$) when in fact it is empty (W$_a$). Either W$_p$ or W$_a$ might be this belief's condition of satisfaction, depending on how the phrase is used. Recall that beliefs are such that, if there is a divergence between W$_p$ and W$_a$, I am obliged to change the belief. Thus the fact that the closet is empty (W$_a$) is the belief's condition of satisfaction, in the sense of the *thing required*. But Searle sometimes talks about W_p, rather than W_a, as its condition of satisfaction: this is the *requirement* (what would be required to be the case, if the belief were to be true). So far as beliefs are concerned, their conditions of satisfaction (requirement) are equivalent to its truth conditions.

Note that these distinctions only hold so far as W_p and W_a diverge. If I have the *true* belief that in 2007 George W. Bush was President of the United States, the content represents the conditions of satisfaction both in the sense of requirement and thing required.

Note that the difficulty does not arise for intentional states with a world-to-mind direction of fit: conditions of satisfaction simply represent W_p.

To conclude, intentional states, for Searle, have two components. First, they have a content, which represents a possible state of affairs or conditions of satisfaction. This representative content makes it possible for an intentional statement to be *about* things. Second, that content serves under a psychological mode that dictates where the problem lies in case of a misfit between the conditions of satisfaction and the world: if the psychological mode is a belief, then the problem lies with the content, but if the psychological mode is a desire, it is the world which needs to be brought in line with the content.

Searle summarizes these two components when he says that, in general, intentional states have the form "*S(r)*," where *S* is the psychological mode and *r* is the representative content.

EXTENDING THE THEORY

Intentional mental states include, but are not limited to the cases of belief and desire. Other states, such as fear, expectation, disappointment, regret, remorse, pride, and shame represent the world by way of either an upward or downward direction of fit. Fear, Searle contends, cannot be reduced to configurations of beliefs and desires—say, the belief that an intruder is in my house and the very strong desire that the intruder be gone. Both of these could be true without entailing that I fear the intruder. Nevertheless, beliefs and desires are paradigm cases of intentionality.[12]

More dramatically, Searle extends his theory of intentionality to umbrella not just beliefs, desires, and other mental states such as fear, but *perception* and *action*. Indeed, there is a certain sense in which belief and desire are not even the paradigm cases of intentionality:

> Beliefs and desires are not the primary forms, rather they are etiolated forms of more primordial experiences in perceiving and doing. Intention, for example, is not a fancy form of desire; it would be more accurate to think of desire as a faded form of intention, intention with the Intentional causation bleached out.[13]

All beliefs, desires, and intentional mental states model or are about the world. Searle describes these cases as etiolated or faded because, as described, the states appear relatively disembodied: they represent possible worlds and the actual world may or may not correspond to them. Beliefs and desires have some bearing on the world as the direction of satisfaction indicates what ought to be fixed in case of a disparity. But this normative imposition on us still understates the sense in which intentional phenomena are *part* of the world, part of the causal mesh leading up to and away from these mental states. Things typically cause us to have beliefs about those things. Desires *can* actualize their conditions of satisfaction. Perception and action are robust, primal cases of this embeddedness, where the world's bringing about a certain content, or else the content bringing about some state of affairs in the world, is not just a possibility, but definitional: perception and action are defined in terms of their realized content.

Perception

A belief's intentional content represents conditions of satisfaction (requirement) to the extent that the conditions of satisfaction diverge from the actual world; the belief is false and needs to be changed. Perception includes visual experience which, like the content of belief, represents a set of conditions of satisfaction. Both contents represent the world under a certain aspect, drawing out certain features while suppressing others. Copernicus' model represents the universe, but the universe under the aspect of celestial movement. As such it is merely globally inaccurate.

Just as the content of a belief can be wrong—it represents conditions of satisfaction or a possible world which does not resemble the actual world—so can visual experiences misrepresent the world. The most vivid example of this is a hallucination, whose conditions of satisfaction represent, for example, an oasis in the desert when in fact there is nothing but sand. I can similarly have a false belief about the existence of an oasis.

Both perceptions and beliefs have a mind-to-world direction of fit, so that in case there is a disparity between the represented conditions of satisfaction (requirement) and the way that the world in fact is, the fault lies with the content. Contrawise, a desire whose content concerns a desert oasis, finds fault with the world, so that the content is only satisfied if we, say, act to build such an oasis. Also, both beliefs and perceptions are identified in terms of their constitutive content or visual experience, so that my saying "I see an oasis" need not imply that there is an oasis.

Against this background of similarities, we are now in a position to discuss the principle point of difference between beliefs and perceptions. Where the content of beliefs represent the conditions of satisfaction in a way that does not require direct acquaintance with its object, visual experience relates to its conditions of satisfaction in a way which is direct, immediate, and involuntary. The basic idea is that the content of a belief can represent a desert as having an oasis, and that belief will be true depending on whether the desert does in fact have an oasis. But a veridical or true perception requires more than (1) a visual experience whose conditions of satisfaction include an oasis and (2) there actually being an oasis that would satisfy its conditions of satisfaction. The visual experience's conditions of satisfaction must also (3) represent the actual oasis as being the cause of the visual experience. Searle describes this third requirement in terms of the content of visual experience being "causally self-referential." The idea is that a belief about the oasis may be true whether or not its content is caused by its object. Not so with perception. A perception of an oasis is not veridical, even if there is an oasis, unless that experience is further caused by the oasis (and is not some optical effect).

This causal immediacy moves Searle to sometimes talk of a visual experience not just *representing* its conditions of satisfaction, but *presenting* those conditions of satisfaction. This distinction emphasizes the way in which perception, for Searle, must be directly caused by its conditions of satisfaction if it is to be veridical.

Perceptions and beliefs are further distinguished on several other grounds.

First, Searle stipulates that "perception," unlike "belief," is a success term. One can have a false belief, but one cannot have a perception which isn't veridical (caused by the very thing its conditions of satisfaction represent). In that way, "perception" semantically functions in a way that is more akin to "knowledge" than "belief." Searle's deployment of the term is potentially confusing as it breaks the analogy with the notion of belief.

Second, the content of beliefs need not be conscious, whereas visual experiences must necessarily be conscious.[14] This has the effect of excluding the so-called "blind sight cases" from the sphere of perception. In these quasi-subliminal cases, a person behaves as if something was seen, but did not have a visual experience of the object.[15]

Third, while both beliefs and perceptions represent their conditions of satisfaction under a certain aspect (are globally inaccurate), because the perception is comprised of a conscious visual experience, that aspect more specifically concerns the point of view of the perceiver and the world's spatiotemporal features. Notice that the aspect under which Copernicus' belief or model represents the universe is not from any particular point of view.

Action

In Chapter 4 we will outline Searle's account of action. Briefly and intuitively, Searle defines action in terms of its causes, so that in order for a body movement to count as an action it must be brought about by beliefs and desires (or other intentional states). Because these beliefs, desires, and other possible mental states (such as fear or shame) are intentional states, and body movements which are actions *must* be caused by such states, Searle extends the concept of the intentional to include the body movements themselves. Indeed, as we saw in the case of perception, there is a certain sense in which actions are more properly intentional than the states which give rise to the associated behavior.

Like perception, the principle difference between desire and action is that the action is causally self-referential. Where a desire's content represents a possible state of affairs (its conditions of satisfaction), the notion of an action further includes the requirement that the content itself bring about those possible states of affairs. This is just the requirement that the beliefs and desires involved in raising my hand cause my hand to rise.

Action is thus necessarily intentional: all actions *must* be preceded by a set of intentional states, such as beliefs and desires. Entities like thermostats and amoebas, which are not capable of sustaining intentionality, are thus incapable of acting (although they are capable of mere behavior). In Chapter 5, we will begin to discuss Searle's philosophy of language. According to Searle, *speech acts* are the fundamental units of language. Because the notion of action is necessarily intentional, this concept of action, discussed in Chapter 4, bridges Searle's philosophy of mind and his philosophy of language.

CHAPTER 4

REASON AND ACTION

We can locate our behavior on a scale that begins with body movements that happen to us and ends with those that we make happen. Coughing, tripping over something, and startle responses might be thus distinguished from waving at someone to get their attention, or saying hello, or even simply raising my arm. The latter are voluntary in ways that the former are not. Between these extremes is a range of intermediary behaviors—breathing, for example, is something that we have a limited amount of control over.

Philosophers of action attempt to say what distinguishes full-blooded action from those behaviors which are involuntary or less voluntary. If we confine our attention just to the behavior itself, the action may seem indistinguishable from a body movement which is not the agent's own. In articulating the puzzle, Searle paraphrases Ludwig Wittgenstein in asking: if I raise my arm, what is left over if I subtract the fact that my arm went up?[1]

Almost all commentators agree that actions can be distinguished from other varieties of body movements in that actions happen intentionally, for a reason. An action's connection to some mental event, intention, or reason, screens it off from body movements that we are reluctant to characterize as actions. Along these lines, Donald Davidson—a principal discussant in the action literature—writes, "Central to the relation between a reason and an action it explains is the idea that the agent performed the action *because* he had the reason."[2] But there remains sharp disagreement over how we ought to interpret the claim that actions are explained by appeal to the reasons had by an agent. Davidson that if an agent performs an action *because* he had a reason, the significance of this claim will remain "dark" until "we can account for the force of that 'because.'"[3]

What is Davidson getting at here? An agent acts because he has a reason, but the subordinating conjunction ("because") that connects action and reason is notoriously slippery. "Because" might be interpreted in at least three not entirely distinct, senses.[4]

THREE SENSES OF THE WORD "BECAUSE"

The word "because" is often used inferentially, so that we can adduce something, which is otherwise hidden, from manifest signs. I may infer that a friend is sick because he is coughing and wheezing. His coughing and wheezing are only symptoms of having influenza, as someone may have the flu and yet not be coughing and wheezing. But the symptoms, which are easy to recognize, are typically reliable enough for me to infer something that would otherwise be difficult to detect—the presence of a virus in the respiratory tract. In using "because" inferentially, we justify why we believe what we do. But there is another mode of justification, which is likewise flagged by the subordinating conjunction. Sometimes I justify a course of action, as when I explain to a traffic officer that I was speeding because I was late. The traffic officer, in turn, cites the law to justify his giving me a ticket. Whether we give reasons for beliefs or actions, we'll call the justificatory use of the subordinating conjunction, "because$_j$." Note that this use need not imply that the justification is *good*. The importance of this sense of the word "because," so far as Searle is concerned, will become clear later in the chapter.

There are two other senses of the word "because" that might be distinguished from "because$_j$."

"Because" may also be used to denote a causal relationship between various events in the world. Someone might point out that the roof collapsed because of the heavy rains or that the car accident occurred because a bush obscured the driver's ability to see oncoming traffic. Such uses of the subordinating conjunction ("because$_e$," where "e" stands for "etiological") endeavor to causally explain one event by appeal to causally antecedent events.[5] We might thus causally explain the expulsion of a political incumbent by appeal to dissatisfaction among religious voters. "Because$_e$" maps objectively real, law-like or quasi law-like relations between two or more events, and has nothing to do with the legitimacy of our beliefs or actions. The relation mapped by the subordinating conjunction is ontological rather than epistemic.

Finally, there is a sense of the word "because" that is neither justificatory, nor causally explanatory, but rather clarificatory. The clarificatory use ("because$_c$") does not seek to justify, nor does it articulate a nomological connection found in the world, but rather aims to illuminate what we *mean*. If I say, "The house is too small *because* the builder misread the plans," I am using the subordinating conjunction in the causally explanatory sense of the word—the misreading explains how the house came to be as small as it is. But contrast this with the claim, "The house is too small *because* there is no room for the grand piano."[6] In this case I am clarifying what it is for the house to be too small; someone else might complain that the house is too small because there are not enough bedrooms for the children. There not being enough bedrooms for the children does not *cause* the house to be too small, in the way that the builder's misreading of the plans might. This statement rather provides an interpretation of a claim that might not otherwise be understood—namely the sense in which the house is too small. Not having enough bedrooms or not being able to accommodate the piano is, in this case, what *counts as* being too small.

Note that in this example, "because$_c$" can be distinguished from "because$_j$." While there is a context in which I could be construed as *justifying* why I think the house is too small, there are also contexts in which I am simply saying what I mean by "small." I might say "he is a bachelor because he is unmarried" to a child who does not yet understand the word. Here I am not justifying why I think someone is a bachelor. A speaker and a hearer must use words in the same way before justification is even possible.

A central disagreement in the philosophy of action can be brought to light by understanding the difference between the causal and the clarificatory senses of the word "because." Recall Davidson's requirement that in order to understand what an action is, we must "account for the force of that 'because'" that links behavior and reasons. Elizabeth Anscombe championed the view that actions and reasons are linked by the noncausalist, *clarificatory* sense of the word "because." But in 1963 Davidson ushered the introduction of a new orthodoxy, wherein actions came to be seen, not as clarified, but as *causally explained* by reasons.

ANSCOMBE ON THE FORCE OF THE "BECAUSE$_c$"

Davidson's causalist account is, in many ways, the more straightforward of the two views. In Davidson's groundbreaking paper, the obscurity of Anscombe's view was cited as a principal reason to endorse the Aristotelean, "common-sense" view that reasons *cause* actions. "I would urge" Davidson writes, "that failing a satisfactory alternative, the best argument for a scheme like Aristotle's is that it alone promises to give an account of the 'mysterious connection' between reasons and actions."[7]

But Anscombe's view is not nearly as mysterious as Davidson suggests. Anscombe agrees with the claim that one acts because one has a reason, and that having a reason distinguishes cases of action from other varieties of body movement. But in placing a reason at the right of the subordinating conjunction, we are *not* thereby citing an event which is causally antecedent to the action in question. If I say "The coffee is good because$_c$ it is not bitter," I am not saying that lack of bitterness *causally explains* the coffee's goodness or even necessarily justifies why I think the coffee is good; I am rather specifying the *way* in which this particular coffee is good.

Anscombe prompts us to reflect on the ordinary situations where we find ourselves puzzled about the significance of someone's behavior (which, like the sounds that come out of our mouths, may be meaningful). Off in the distance a man, walking by a tree, begins to maniacally flail his arms. In this concrete situation we might be puzzled about the significance of the behavior. We might ask of him, "Why were you waving so violently?" If he responds, "I waved my hands because$_c$ I wanted to get your attention," he is clarifying the significance of his action: by moving his arms he *meant* "look over here." To be able to cite a reason, in Anscombe's view, entails the ability to clarify or rearticulate the significance of the event—thunderstorms do not happen for a reason precisely because they are not normally the sort of thing of which we can demand an interpretation.

A common way to reject a request for clarification or reinterpretation is to answer a different kind of why-question. Our interlocutor might, for example, do this by providing a causal history of the body movement—"I waved my hands because$_e$ the cobweb startled me."[8] There is no answer to the *clarificatory* why-question as the behavior is, we discover, like the thunder storm, not the sort of thing for which we can demand clarification or interpretation; the behavior, in short, is found not to be an action. All actions, for Anscombe, are capable of being interpreted, clarified, or elucidated. When bank robber Willie Sutton was asked why he robbed banks he famously responded, "Because$_e$ that is where the money is."[9] His response, in effect, was a rejection of the question which, presumably, sought an interpretation or clarification of these actions. If he had answered *that* question, he might have said that he robbed banks because$_c$ he intended to comment on the ruthlessness of American capitalism, or to express a kind of internal rage, or whatnot. Part of what is so chilling about his response is the implied possibility that human behavior is more akin to a force of nature than something we meaningfully do.

Note that Anscombe is not denying that actions are caused by mental states. She is rather pointing out that when we look at the ordinary case where interpretive disambiguation is required, to cite a cause is often tantamount to denying that the behavior is the sort of thing that even could be clarified. A mental state may precede an action, but when it comes to why-questions which are requests for clarification, she denies that "it is in itself of very great importance."[10] Also, as indicated above, there is an intimate, but not necessary link between clarifications and justifications. Anscombe exploits this link to show how clarifications can often also be construed as reasons for action.

DAVIDSON ON THE FORCE OF THE "BECAUSE$_E$"

Anscombe thinks the fact that a body movement may be brought about by certain mental causes is irrelevant to the determination of whether or not that body movement is an action. For her, an action just is the kind of body movement which can be interpreted or clarified; it is the sort of thing that can be misunderstood. By contrast Davidson thinks that certain body movements are actions because the movements are brought about in the right way. A body movement's causal history is, thus, of tremendous importance for Davidson. Body movements that can be traced to beliefs and desires (what he calls "primary reasons") are actions; otherwise, the body movements are, at best, reactions. The flailing of arms was an action if a causal trail can be drawn from his desire to draw our attention to the behavior; the arm movements fail to be an action if it was largely a blind response to running into a spider web.

When Davidson claims that we act because we have reasons, he understands "because" in the ordinary, causal sense of the word. Indeed, he seems to go so far as to suggest that there is no other way to understand the subordinating conjunction.[11]

For better or for worse, Davidson's view has long established itself as orthodoxy in the philosophy of action. Searle's own views on action are largely Davidsonian (Searle and Davidson were colleagues at the University of California at Berkeley).

SEARLE'S ACCOUNT OF ACTION IN *INTENTIONALITY*

Searle's account of action, at least as presented in *Intentionality*, is largely Davidsonian, as both distinguish actions from other body movements by appeal to the fact that actions have a mental cause.

Both Davidson and Searle require that every action has what Searle calls, in *Rationality in Action*, a "motivator."[12] A paradigm case of a motivator is a desire. If I have a desire to eat ice cream, this is what motivates me to do so. Of course, each action (such as eating ice cream) is further enabled or made possible by means of a series of beliefs: in order to satisfy my desires, I must correctly believe, for example, that ice cream is to be found in the freezer rather than in the pantry. But desires, as well as other kinds of motivators, are what ultimately impel action; they contain, within the representative content, the *point* of the resulting behavior. Without desires, for example, action would be impossible—that is, there would be no reason to move an arm or make a sound. In Chapter 9 we will see that Searle allows for "desire-independent" motivators, as when we act for moral reasons or else from duties and obligations.

Differences between Davidson's and Searle's accounts of action can, of course, be found in the details. For example, while Davidson describes mental causes in terms of beliefs and desires (primary reasons), Searle prefers the more inclusive notion of intentionality. Recall from Chapter 3, that beliefs and desires are intentional, but not all intentional states (such as fear) can be reduced to configurations of beliefs and desires. In a latter paper, Davidson concedes that intentions cannot be reduced to beliefs and desires.[13]

Searle expands Davidson's account by suggesting that a body movement's mental cause—what he calls an "intention in action"— may itself be caused by another kind of intention, the "prior intention."[14] This is not a fundamental departure from Davidson's account, but the addition of a prior mental cause does help Searle avoid the so-called "deviant causal chain" puzzle.

In order for behavior to count as an action, the intentionality which brings about the behavior must be causally self-referential: the intentions must cause its conditions of satisfaction, the bodily movements. But while this is a necessary condition, it is not sufficient: philosophers have worried about cases in which the beliefs and desires bring about the intended behavior in the *wrong way*. R. M. Chisholm imagines a case where someone intends to kill his uncle. He sets out in his car to do just that. But he is so distracted by the prospect of killing his uncle that he fails to see someone in the road, and so runs him over. The pedestrian, further, happens to be his uncle. In this case the intention to kill his uncle caused the killing of his uncle; but in spite of the connection, this killing is not an action.[15] Philosophers are tasked with explaining the difference between genuine acts of murder and this degenerate case; the difference cannot be simply that the act of murder is caused by some intention or desire.

It is with this puzzle in mind that Searle introduces the distinction between prior intentions and intentions in action. The man's running over his uncle is not a case of murder because, while he had the prior intention to kill his uncle, and this prior intention brought about the uncle's death, it did not do so by way of an intention in action. Consider the contrasting case. The man sets out with the (prior) intention of killing his uncle. He sees his uncle crossing the road which leads him to steer intentionally into his victim. This second "intention in action" is the one that matters in distinguishing genuine actions from those consequences which result from inattentive driving. This is a case of genuine murder, an action; the behavior is caused not just by some intention or other, but by an intention in action.

Searle solves the problem of deviant causal chains by suggesting that while the driver had a prior intention to kill his uncle, he did not do so with the requisite intention in action. This explains why we are not tempted to charge the driver with first degree murder.[16]

It is not uncommon for a prior intention to eventually cause me to act in a particular way. But it is not necessary that the action be in accordance with that prior intention. For example, I might have the prior intention to vote for candidate A in an election. Upon situating myself in the voting booth, I have a sudden change of heart and vote for candidate B. The fact that this action was not in accord with a prior intention does not mean I did not act—this is not a case of someone's forcing my hand to vote for candidate B or a case of my accidentally checking candidate B because my hand cramped at the last moment. The vote is still an action because the body movement can be traced, if not to a prior intention, to the intention in action which constituted my change of heart. Even in the case where I voted for candidate A, my action is an action, not because I had the prior intention to vote for A, but because the body movement can be traced to an intention in action to vote for A; the prior intention, in this case, was only the cause of the intention in action—the one that matters in distinguishing actions from mere body movements.

Another difference between Davidson's and Searle's accounts of action concerns the extension of the word "action." For Davidson, "action" refers to a type of body movement—namely, those which are appropriately caused by certain mental states. Searle stipulates that the word "action" covers not just the body movement, but also the intention which causes it. The difference between these two senses is trivial. Davidson's use does not refer to any body movement, but *only* those body movements that are caused by mental states. Searle, recognizing that the causal history is an essential ingredient of the notion, decides to explicitly include those mental states (intentions in action) under the umbrella of the term.

Davidson's account of action may be schematized as in Figure 4.1:

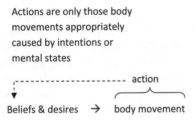

Actions are only those body movements appropriately caused by intentions or mental states

The overall picture presented by Searle is as seen in Figure 4.2:

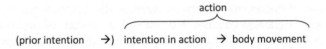

The difference is nominal, differing over whether "action" is predicated over the behavior (which in both cases must be caused by the intention) or the intention-behavior pairing. Consider "stumbling." In order to stumble there must be an exogenous cause, whether or not that cause is denoted by "stumble." The Oxford English Dictionary defines "stumble" as follows: "To miss one's footing, or trip over an obstacle, in walking or running, so as to fall or be in danger of falling." Does "stumble" refer to the case of your body's falling forward (prompted by your having hit an obstacle)? Or does it refer to a combination of hitting something and then falling forward? Indeed, is there a genuine philosophical problem of stumbling here? There is not—there is just a narrow and wider use of the word, both of which are made true or false by the same sequence of events.

Note that Davidson's use of the term is probably more in line with our ordinary understanding; when we speak of someone acting, we typically have *only* their body movements in mind, even if we grant that it is the case that those body movements must be caused by some intention or other.

To conclude, in accounting "for the force of that 'because'" which links action and intention, Searle follows Davidson in recommending that the "because" is causal. Actions are simply those behaviors that are causally connected to intentional states such as beliefs and desires.

SEARLE'S ACCOUNT OF ACTION IN *RATIONALITY IN ACTION*

Rationality in Action (2001) builds on the basic causalist account of action as found in *Intentionality* (1983) to more sharply diverge from Davidson's view. "Because" links actions and intentions, but Searle's mature view denies that the subordinating conjunction can be construed exclusively in terms of causation ("because$_e$"). In particular, Searle argues that the "because" must also include a justificatory element ("because$_j$").

Searle begins by arguing against those—including Davidson—who view the link between intentions and behavior as *simply* causal. He calls the causalist account "the Classical Model."

Because beliefs and desires are causally efficacious, it is tempting to push the analogy between these and other varieties of causal antecedents. Consider the following examples of causation. First, the rain falls and collects on the branches and leaves of a water oak, causing one of the older branches to break and fall. Second, someone forcibly manipulates my arm into a raised position. Third, I willfully and intentionally raise my arm. The first and second effects are distinguished from the third case in that the first and second effects were not the (direct) result of an intentional cause.

According to the regularity theory of causation, whose advocates include Hume, any time certain conditions are satisfied—the branch is not overly thick, the cellular structure has been weakened with age, gravity is present, a certain amount of water has collected, and so on—it is *invariably* the case that the branch will fall. Similarly, if someone grasps my arm with sufficient force and applies sufficient pressure, assuming there are no obstacles, my arm *must* rise. Note that any one of these conditions is not sufficient to break the branch or raise my arm. If water accumulates on the branch, but it is relatively thick or else resting on another branch, it will not fall. If the attempted manipulation of my arm is cancelled out by my own strength, it will not rise. But if the weight of the water or the upward force of the push is complemented by a series of other conditions, then the regularity theory of causation holds that these *must always* eventuate in the aforementioned effects. That is, according to this model of causation, every effect is nomologically necessitated by some earlier state; if those initial conditions are replicated, the same kind of effect is bound to result.

Looking at the third case, wherein I choose to raise my arm, regularity theorists might likewise contend that a constellation of beliefs and desires (or other intentional states) are such that they entail or necessitate my arm's going up. Anyone with the same beliefs and desires would, all things being equal, invariably raise their arm. Like causes are followed by like effects, even within the realm of intentional, agentive causation.

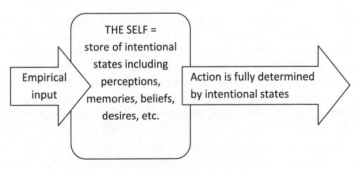

The Classical Model's (Hume; Regularity Theory) account of self and its relation to action

While Searle endorses the regularity theory of causation as applied to nonintentional phenomena,[17] he strongly disagrees with those who would extend it to the case of intentional causation. The Classical Model sees action as a kind of vector which results from the combined forces of an agent's various beliefs and desires. These various intentional contents are causally sufficient for action. Searle does not deny that such contents are among an action's causal antecedents, but denies that any action can be fully, sufficiently explained by appeal to intentional contents.

There are, of course, times when our mental states *do* fully compel action—as when we cannot help ourselves in the face of a particularly strong or intractable desire. Addiction, love, or fear might induce an experience such that we feel subject to those intentional states. We might, in these cases, have the experience of standing outside of ourselves or watching ourselves being acted on rather than acting. But these are atypical, degenerate cases of acting. Searle's principle complaint with the Classical Model is that it has the effect of elevating these exceptional cases to the paradigm case.

But in rational cases of action, if our beliefs and desires are not causally sufficient conditions for action, what causes, for example, my hand to go up?

The simple answer is that *I do*. I am not, contra Hume, *simply* a bundle of intentional states. In particular the self includes both volitional and cognitive components. The volitional component wills or initiates action; Searle calls this part of the self the "agent." Agency is causally sufficient to bring about certain bodily movements. But the important thing to see is that this mode of causation does not appear to be necessitated by extant conditions in the world, be they beliefs and desires, or neural-biological configurations. But neither is volition a case of causation *ex nihilo*, which is causally insensitive to the world. An action is willed, not simply by virtue of a set of beliefs and desires, but in *consultation with* those beliefs and desires. That is, while beliefs and desires do not causally necessitate a course of action, as per the regulatory theory of causation, they still may be said to cause and justify an action. Thus full selves include, not just the capacity for agency or volition, but clusters of beliefs, desires, perceptions, memories, and other intentional states. Moreover, these various intentional contents and volitional faculties must be gathered within a unified field which flags these as the agent's own.

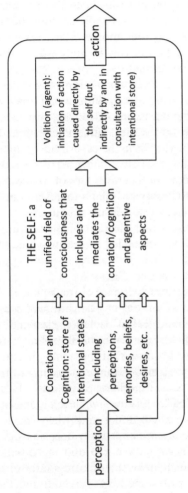

Searle's account of self and its relation to action

The Classical Model of action has several advantages over Searle's. It is more elegant and much easier to reconcile with Searle's own commitment to Scientific Naturalism. However, as we have seen, it misses one vital feature: it cannot account for the experience of acting. In raising my arm I do not feel as though this is something to which I am subject. My own beliefs and desires do not typically compel my arm in the same way that another human being could or in the way that an accumulation of rain causes a branch to fall. In spite of the Classical Model's theoretical virtues, it runs exactly counter to our own, undeniable experience of psychological freedom—being able to decide how we are to act. Without the experience of psychological freedom, the experience of moving my own arm would be uncomfortably close to the experience of having my arm moved or manipulated, except the acting forces would be endogenous rather than exogenous. But even when confronted with a desire to do something which does not conflict with any other desire, we retain the sense that we can do otherwise. We may decide to act on that desire, and in doing so we can cite the desire as both a cause and a reason of the action; but in saying that the desire was a cause, we do not imply that we were somehow compelled to action. Thus, so far as actions are concerned, while beliefs and desires are among the causes of an action, they are not causally sufficient.

Of course, perhaps the experience of freedom is an illusion. In that case Searle's model of action, at best, articulates how words such as "self," "action," and "reason" function grammatically within the English language. If freedom is an illusion, Searle's model is ontologically inert. We will consider this possibility below.

According to Searle's model, the principle motivation for the postulation of the self is the experience of freedom. This freedom takes place within what Searle calls the *gap*: "the gap is that feature of our conscious decision making and acting where we sense alternative future decisions and actions as causally open to us."[18]

The self operates within the gap and in consultation with the intentional store, but remains a sufficient source of action. In fact, between the desire to do something and the completion of an action there are *three* gaps or points at which the self can intervene. In consultation with the intentional store, the self arrives at a decision to act in a way that is sensitive to an agent's beliefs and desires (prior intentions), then decides to act (intentions in action), acts, and then brings the act to completion.[19] Because the initial decision is sensitive

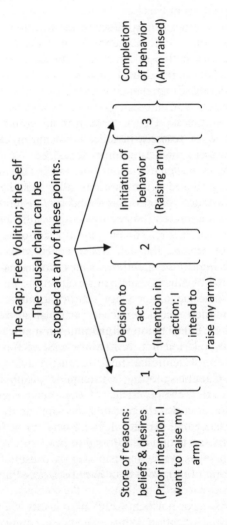

to an agent's particular constellation of beliefs and desires, these are causal factors. But because volition may nevertheless abort the chain of events that begins with a set of beliefs and desires, and ends with the completion of the action, the beliefs and desires may not be said to be causally sufficient.

We are now in a position to describe the transition from Searle's earlier account of action as found in *Intentionality*, to his more mature account of action as found in *Rationality in Action*. While most philosophers agree that actions happen *because* of reasons, there is considerable disagreement over the sense in which the subordinating conjunction must be understood. As we have seen, in *Intentionality* Searle follows Davidson in recommending that actions happen because$_e$ of reasons; in order for behavior to count as an action it is must be *caused* by intentional states.

To be clear, in *Rationality in Action*, Searle still maintains that actions must be caused by intentional states; thus, he continues to endorse the account of action as found in *Intentionality*. But he denies that these intentional states are causally sufficient for, or even proximal causes of, action. The proper, sufficient cause of an action is the *self*. But because the self acts in consultation with various beliefs and desires, those intentional states or reasons are not causally inert. So there remains a sense in which actions happen because$_e$ of intentions in action, as per Searle's earlier account.

However, Searle's reconsidered view adds an additional way in which actions are linked to intentional states: not only are beliefs and desires causally relevant but they can be used to further *justify* or *warrant* an action. Intentional states that justify an action have normative force. Caught speeding, I attempt to justify my action by appealing to my desire not to be late: "I was speeding because$_j$ I didn't want to be late." It is also the case that this same desire *caused* me to speed: "I was speeding because$_e$ I didn't want to be late." But not every cause of some action can be used to justify the action: the fact that my tank had gas in it was also among the causes of my speeding (without it's being full I would not have been speeding), but it does not warrant my speeding.

There are two ways in which X can fail to justify Y. First, X can be a *bad* reason or justification. While being late is not a great reason to speed, the fact that one's hair needs to be blown dry is a positively bad reason to speed. However, X can fail to justify Y in a more severe sense. Y or X may not be the kind of things that can stand in a justificatory relation in the first place. X, in this case, might not even count as a *bad justification* of Y. I'll use the word "unjustifiable" to flag phenomena which are not even candidates for justification, good or bad.

Consider three instances in which Y is unjustifiable. Typically, although not always, the thing being justified must be an action. Something can be an unjustifiable Y, then, if that Y is not an action. For example, the rain causally explains why a branch fell, but doesn't justify its falling. The problem, here, is not that the rain badly justifies the branch's falling. Rather, rain and branches are not the sort of things that can stand in a justificatory relationship in the first place; they are unjustifiable. An analogous case is one where someone physically forces my arm up. My behavior is unjustifiable. But, in this case, my arm going up is not an action.

Searle's innovation is to suggest that there are also some *actions* which are also unjustifiable.

An addict shoots heroin because of a desire to feel pleasure. This is an action, according to both Searle and Davidson, because the behavior is caused by intentions in action. But the desire to feel pleasure fails to justify the heroin shot. As stated, the significance of this claim is left ambiguous. It could mean simply that the desire to feel pleasure is not a *good* justification; the addict has other, better reasons to not shoot heroin. But now imagine that the addict is severely, blindly addicted: the desire for heroin has totally eclipsed these competing motivators so that he or she *cannot help* but pursue the drug. Notice that for the superaddict, the shooting of heroin remains an action—it is behavior caused by intentions in action. But the action is *unjustifiable*. It is not the sort of event that could be justified. It is not that the action is done for *bad* reasons, but—like the fallen tree limb—it is not the sort of thing for which a justification, good or bad, could be given. The shooting of heroin, in this case, is more like a blind force of nature, whose causes cannot be traced back to a self.

Given the Searle-Davidson definition of action, what distinguishes rational actions from irrational actions? Irrational actions are compelled from within; these are actions that couldn't be otherwise, as by way of an overwhelming desire. While such actions are caused by intentional states, they are otherwise akin to natural phenomena. Such incidents typically displace the agent from the sphere of accountability, as under the legal concept of diminished capacity. Irrational actions are those that are easily brought under the standard,

regularity theory of causation. Searle remarks with some astonish-
ment that the Classical Model of action ends up endorsing as
paradigm a variety of actions that would normally be thought of as
irrational.

> I want to say that cases of actions for which the antecedent beliefs
> and desires really are causally sufficient, far from being models of
> rationality, are in fact bizarre and typically irrational cases. These
> are the cases where, for example, the agent is in the grip of an
> obsession or an addiction and cannot do otherwise than to act
> upon his desire. But in a typical case of rational decision making
> where, for example, I am trying to decide which candidate to vote
> for, I have a choice and I consider various reasons for choosing
> among the alternatives available to me. But I can only engage in
> this activity if I assume that my set of beliefs and desires by itself
> is not causally sufficient to determine my action.[20]

Rational actions, then, are simply those where one is able to otherwise act, even given an identical configuration of intentional states.
If I want to eat and need to eat, but decide not to, my action, although
badly justified, remains rational. It is rational precisely because I was
not internally or externally compelled to behave in a certain way.

Searle's considered view is as follows. In order to count as an action,
a behavior must be caused by intentions in action, which include
beliefs and desires. But not all actions are rational. Rational actions
are those where the intentions in action do *not* necessitate or guaran-
tee one behavior or another. Actions which stem from overwhelming
intentional states, such as drug addiction, are not rational; they are
unjustifiable. Rational actions are caused by the self, in consultation
with one's intentional states. Rational actions are thus caused by
intentional states, without being determined by those same states.

Just to be clear, not all rational actions are, further, justified
(although all justified actions are rational). Justified actions do not
just happen in consultation with intentional states, but are optimally
executed by way of some standard. Someone who attempts to lose
weight by strictly adhering to a diet of french fries may be acting
rationally—they are not in any way *compelled* to eat fast food even
given their desire to lose weight. But the action is badly justified—
such a diet is a poor way to lose weight. As mentioned, there are two
senses in which an action can fail to be justified: it can be unjustified

in that I am acting for *bad* reasons. Or it can be unjustifiable, in that my action is not the sort of event for which any reasons—good or bad—can be proffered. Unjustifiable actions are irrational and imply compulsion or some kind or other. Mere behavior is likewise unjustifiable.

Searle's emphasis between *Intentionality* and *Rationality in Action* has thus changed. As in *Intentionality*, he still believes that actions are caused by intentional states (because$_e$). However, with the introduction of genuine agency, actions and reasons now stand in two relations: while the causal link between intentional states and actions hold, those intentional states can, further, justify or rationalize those actions. Indeed, actions are not simply behavior that has the right causal pedigree; actions are typically the sort of events which can be justified (or fail to be justified, in the weak sense). And this is only possible if action is something that is willed by a self. Contra Davidson, only when intentional states and body movements are mediated by the self (take place in the gap; are rational) can those intentional states properly be said to be *reasons*: action not only happen because$_e$ of reasons, but, more importantly, rational actions happen because$_j$ of reasons.

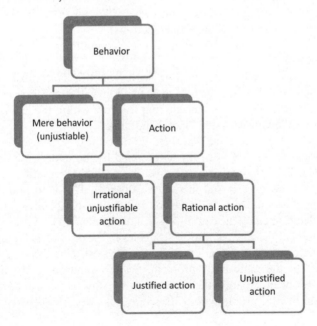

FREEDOM AND SCIENTIFIC NATURALISM:
THE ONTOLOGICAL QUESTION

Given that the gap—the sense of being able to do otherwise—is so radically consistent with our experience in acting, why is the dominant Classical Model committed to a view which seeks to remove, downplay, or reduce this central feature of action? Recall that Searle is a Scientific Naturalist, in that he endorses the view that physics describes the basic constituents of the world. Searle is especially interested in locating various features of the world—mind, language, institutions—within the scope of this foundational ontology. Indeed, he frames a central project of *Rationality in Action* in precisely these terms: "How can there be rational decision making in a world where everything that occurs happens as a result of brute, blind, natural causal forces?"[21] The Classical Model renders rational decision making less puzzling by treating action as just another kind of natural occurrence. However, the experience of the gap suggests a possibility that stands in marked contrast with the basic tenets of a physicalist ontology. Where the world is assumed to be a closed system of causes, and like causes are assumed to produce like effects, the gap suggests that human agency is not physically determined and constitutes a category of causation where like causes (desires) do *not* necessarily manifest in like effects (actions).

Is freedom compatible with Searle's commitment to Scientific Naturalism?

One way to reconcile freedom with Scientific Naturalism is to eliminate or redescribe the notion of freedom within the terms of the physical base. This is to concede that freedom within the gap is illusory or, following Jackson, "merely putative."

Searle also entertains another, more radical strategy. Perhaps volitional causes are not fully determined by the underlying neurobiological or physical substructure. Accordingly, causation within the gap is *sui generis* and metaphysically real. This is to grant that certain effects in the world (actions and their consequences) are not fully determined by the causal-physical net leading up to those events.

Note that these two solution strategies to the ontological question are analogous to those adopted by the physicalists and Searle, with respect to the mind-body problem. Searle's solution to the mind-body problem expands the conception of what is natural so as to include mental events within its scope. Likewise, the theorist who holds freedom to be real, stretches the notion of the natural to include causes that are not themselves fully determined by antecedent events within the physical sphere.

Searle remains carefully agnostic about the veracity of these mutually exclusive solution strategies. If we naturalize freedom, we get an account of the world which is more elegant and simple, but which defies our manifest experience. However, if we stretch the notion of the natural to include the possibility of events—agent causation—which are not fully determined by their causal antecedents, we are left unsettled: "The problem is to see how the consciousness of the system could give it a causal efficacy that is not deterministic."[22] This possibility, which is entailed by any ontologically robust conception of the gap, "does not sit comfortably with our existing conception of biology."[23]

In any case, Searle remains committed to the claim that the grammar or ordinary use of the concept *reason* cannot be reduced to the grammar of the concept *cause*, where effects are assumed to invariably follow from a set of causes. If the notion of a gap marks a metaphysically real phenomenon, while actions may be said to be caused by intentional states, they are not invariably so caused. Rather, an agent simply acts, and appeals to reasons in justifying that action.

CHAPTER 5

FROM ACTS TO SPEECH ACTS:
THE INTENTION TO COMMUNICATE

Searle is perhaps best known for his work in the philosophy of language, which constitutes his earliest writings. While the details of Searle's philosophy of action were worked out later on in his career, much of the apparatus was developed with an eye toward his earlier account of language. Searle's conception of action is continuous with his conception of language precisely because language is always linked with action. The basic unit of language is what Searle calls a "speech act." If several pieces of driftwood collect on the shore of an ocean in the shape of the word "hello," at least part of what precludes this physical event from the sphere of the linguistic is that it was not the result of an agent's beliefs and desires. The waves that caused the pieces of wood to fall in this manner are not prompted by the requisite intentions in action, as required by Searle's account of action:

> When I take a noise or a mark on a piece of paper to be an instance of linguistic communication, as a message, one of the things I must assume is that the noise or mark was produced by a being or beings more or less like myself and produced with certain kinds of intentions.[1]

Note that if a collection of wood composed a Shakespearian sonnet, we might conclude that it is genuinely linguistic. But in doing so, we assume the presence of intentional agency—either that of a trickster or perhaps Divine intervention.[2]

Note that while Searle talks about *speech* acts, there is no essential link between language and the use of the voice. If I pencil the letters "hello," or make certain gestures with my hands, these may also be speech acts.

Language implicates vocal or physical acts. But action is only a necessary but not a sufficient feature of something being language. In boiling an egg, or humming a melody, or moving a chess piece, I am acting, but I am not, further, engaged in speech. What distinguishes speech acts from other kinds of (rational) action?

The quick, but so far uninformative answer, is that speech acts are *meaningful* in a way that boiling an egg, humming, or moving a chess piece are not. Consider the following limiting case of the difference between speech acts and other kinds of action: imagine two people who intentionally utter the sounds "Jones went home," but only the first of whom *means* what they have said. Perhaps the second does not know English and is mimicking the first. What makes only the first utterance, not just an action, but a speech action?

This question can be phrased in the form of a philosophical conundrum. Parroting the question we asked regarding what differentiates action from mere behavior, the philosopher of language might query: if he spoke meaningfully, what is left over if I subtract the fact that he spoke? To put it another way, consider ordinary sentences such as "It is raining" or "I promise to cash the check" against the Scientific Naturalist's ontological backdrop. What is perplexing to the Scientific Naturalist are not the *noises* made—sounds are, after all, nothing but a range of frequencies. Rather, the feature of our words and sentences that is not easily reconciled with our naturalistic account of the world is the fact that they are meaningful. The mechanical vibrations which constitute sound have a well-understood scientific basis, but meaning does not. In this vein, Searle asks, "How is it possible, for example, that when I say 'Jones went home,' which after all is in one way just a string of noises, what I mean is: Jones went home. What is the difference between saying something and meaning it and saying it without meaning it?"[3]

TWO CONCEPTIONS OF MEANING: SPEECH ACTS AND THE COMMUNICATION-INTENTION THEORISTS

Before we can answer the question as to how meaning is possible (the ontological question), we have to get clearer on what meaning *is* for Searle.

Peter Strawson, in "Meaning and Truth," describes a "Homeric struggle" between two philosophical conceptions of meaning.[4] On the one hand there are the *semanticists*, who trace their own tradition to Gotlobb Frege, Bertrand Russell, and the early Ludwig Wittgenstein. On the other hand, there are the *communication-intention theorists*, who look to G. E. Moore, the later Wittgenstein, John Austin, and Paul Grice for inspiration. To understand where Searle fits into this dichotomy, it is necessary to have a clear sense of the views and motivations which underlie both of these traditions.

Meaning, for the semanticist, is principally found in a word's capacity to refer to the world, to describe it as being a certain way. If I say, "It is raining in New York," that sentence's meaning is found in its truth conditions: this sentence represents New York as under storm clouds. Truth conditions are the semantic counterpart to Searle's notion of conditions of satisfaction (requirement)—a connection to which we will return below. Strawson, in characterizing the semanticist, writes "the thought that the sense of a sentence is determined by its truth-conditions is to be found in Frege and in the early Wittgenstein, and we find it again in many subsequent writers."[5] As the early Wittgenstein says, words are pictures and "the picture is a model of reality."[6] When a sentence is true, the elements of a proposition—its sense—must have a referent. "That is how a picture is attached to reality; it reaches right out to it."[7] While other theorists, such as A. J. Ayer, contend that words directly reach out to reality without a mediating picture, all semanticists endorse the basic idea that words are meaningful because they describe or represent the world. For this reason, utterances such as "Colorless green ideas sleep furiously" or the sounds of wind whistling through a canyon do not qualify as meaningful: they do not represent the world as being a certain way.

Is Searle a semanticist about meaning? We will explore this question in greater detail below, but it is worth pointing out that Searle is relatively sympathetic with this view. As we will see, Searle maintains that linguistic utterances mirror the structure of intentionality. Every intentional state consists of a representative content brought under a psychological mode with one of two directions of fit; the representative content models the world by way of its conditions of satisfaction, and the psychological mode indicates what the thinker is to do in case of a mis-fit between the model and the world. If linguistic utterances turn out to reflect the structure of intentionality and the latter has representative content, then our words will also have a representative content—what Searle calls "propositional content." This propositional content is meaningful in the sense specified by the semanticist—it represents the world as being a certain way.

A principle difficulty with the semanticist conception of language is that it appears to preclude a great deal of what we ordinarily would count as meaningful. The paradigm case of an utterance with truth conditions is a hypothesis, such as "It is raining in New York." But not all speech acts have truth conditions; not all utterances appear to represent the world as being a certain way. The later Wittgenstein, observing that language is a complex phenomenon and is not the sort of thing we should expect to bring under a simple characterization (i.e., whatever has truth conditions). However, our philosophical commitments can dull our sensitivity to the multiplicity of the phenomena which count as meaningful. To remind ourselves of this requires that we review and re-review the mundane circumstances in which words have application. Wittgenstein attempts to break us free from the idea that language principally represents the world by surveying the many ways in which we might be said to use words meaningfully:

> Forming and testing a hypothesis—
> Presenting the results of an experiment in tables and diagrams—
> Making up a story; and reading it—
> Play-acting—
> Singing catches—
> Guessing riddles—
> Making a joke; telling it—
> Solving a problem in practical arithmetic—
> Translating from one language into another—
> Asking, thanking, cursing, greeting, praying.[8]

Wittgenstein draws out this multiplicity by way of a rich metaphor:

> Think of the tools in a tool-box: there is a hammer, pliers, a saw, a screw-driver, a rule, a glue-pot, glue, nails and screws.—The functions of words are as diverse as the functions of these objects. (And in both cases there are similarities.)
> Of course, what confuses us is the uniform appearance of words when we hear them spoken or meet them in script and print.

For their application is not presented to us so clearly. Especially when we are doing philosophy.[9]

Wittgenstein suggests that the semanticist temptation stems from the exercise of looking at the word, as met in script and print, and then looking at objects in the world—perhaps imagining an arrow between them or even that the object has the word inscribed on it. But to do this is *already* to abstract the words from the circumstances in which they acquire their significance, perhaps overstating the centrality of reference. In assenting to the semanticist's conception of meaning, we bring language under an oversimple picture—that linguistic utterances reach out to the world and touch it—and then we find ourselves perplexed when that picture leaves us unable to account for words' manifold functions.

Consider the kind of puzzles that arise if we assume the hypothesis (the indicative case) to be the paradigm case of meaning, as per the semanticist. Much that is written in the philosophy of language is dedicated to showing how nonparadigm cases of language use are in fact derivative of the standard, indicative case. Sentences which contain nonreferring expressions to the present King of France are baffling because the subject seems to refer to something that does not exist. How do words reach out to *that*? How does the semanticist account for irony or sarcasm, where what is *meant* is often the opposite of what is *said*? Moreover, there are a number of speech acts that do not even purport to be descriptions of the world: a builder's order to have an assistant bring building material forth, my saying "hello" to someone, or a promise to pay back money given to me.

For those working within the broad outlines of the semanticist's assumptions, the aim is to disentangle the primary, semantical, expository aspects of language use from the secondary, pragmatic aspects of language, and then to give an explanation as to how the latter is derivative of the former. For the semanticist, semantics—the ability to refer—is always prior to pragmatics.

But these puzzles simply do not arise if, following the later Wittgenstein, we adopt a more inclusive characterization of meaning that *prioritizes* the many things which language can do in addition to describing the world. The *communication-intention theorists* endeavor to do precisely that: privilege pragmatics over semantics.

The communication-intention theorists, such as the later Wittgenstein, Grice, Austin, and Strawson, have observed that, telling jokes, giving hypotheses, ordering, greeting, and making up stories are all forms of *communication*. What all instances of meaningful speech have in common, then, is they are made with the intention of producing some effect or other on an audience. The various kinds of speech acts are thus distinguished according to the *kind* of effect they have on the hearer. Austin called these utterances, which are hearer directed and attempt to affect the audience in a variety of ways according to certain conventions, "performatives." All speech acts, on the model of tools, thus have a functional component: they aim to produce an effect on an audience.

Note that it is not required that the utterance actually succeed in producing this functional effect in order to count as a speech act. A dull knife is still a knife, even if it can't cut. So long as the utterance is made by an agent with the intention to produce the effect, that is sufficient to qualify the act as a speech act. If I say "Jones went home" to someone who does not speak English, I have succeeded in making a speech act, even if I failed to communicate, because I said it with the *intention* to produce understanding, an effect, in the hearer.

Communication is a highly conventional affair; we communicate for contingent purposes according to more or less well-defined rules. "I promise to cash the check" communicates my intention only in virtue of constitutive rules that are shared by both me and my interlocutor. Perhaps we can catalogue the kinds of communication there are by explicating the constitutive rules a person follows in using language. The rules themselves are often embedded into the grammatical form of an utterance, so that the sounds, "Bring the water!" count as an order for water in English, whereas "The water was brought," counts as an assertion. For the communication-intention theorist, rather than the semanticist, Strawson writes, "rules are, precisely, rules for communicating, rules by the observance of which the utterer may achieve his purpose, fulfill his communication-intention; and that this is their *essential* character."[10]

Is Searle a communication-intention theorist? The early Searle takes it for granted that linguistic meaning is best explicated according to what can be *done* with words, according to what effect can be produced by them. At least he explicitly characterizes himself as working within the boundaries of Austin's communication-intention framework (Searle was Austin's student at Oxford). Searle writes that, "My earliest work was in the philosophy of language, and a good deal of it was an attempt to develop a general theory of speech acts. I made extensive use of insights already developed by other Oxford philosophers, especially Austin."[11]

In *Speech Acts* Searle explicitly states that his account of meaning follows Grice's, another communication-intention theorist: "In speaking I attempt to communicate certain things to my hearer by getting him to recognize my intention to communicate just those things."[12] What is important to see here is that Searle defines meaning in terms of the effect an utterance can have on the hearer: we say something and mean it, just in case I attempt to communicate things to my hearer. The key ingredient which distinguishes speech from other kinds of action is, then, that speech is done with the intention of communicating, of producing understanding in the hearer. In boiling an egg, I am acting, but I am not eliciting understanding in a hearer. But, for example, "hello" is meaningful just in case I try to produce in the hearer a certain effect—namely, the knowledge that I am greeting them. This example is also nice in that "hello" does not appear to have representational content, and so cannot easily be brought under the semanticist picture. We will rehearse the details of Searle's full account of meaning below.

Part of the force of Searle's contending that the speech act, rather than the word or sentence, is the fundamental unit of language, is that language is causally embedded into the world. The linguistic is a relational fact, defined across a temporal continuum: it is produced by an agent, in response to certain intentions and states of affairs in the world, in order to bring about certain results. But according to the semanticist, words essentially have senses and those senses refer to the world as though hovering timelessly above it. For the semanticist, the fact that an agent uses words to communicate is regarded as a derivative, pragmatic feature of the linguistic. But if speech is an act, then language is always something that is done by an agent, for various purposes. These purposes are enshrined in the actor's conditions of satisfaction, and the realization of those purposes is found in the effects brought about by such acts. Where the semanticist sees the referential component of language as logically prior to the pragmatic component, Searle, in *Speech Acts*, contends that the order of priority is in fact exactly the opposite:

a study purely of those formal [semantic and syntactic] features, without a study of their role in speech acts, would be like a formal study of the currency and credit systems of economies without a study of the role of currency and credit in economic transactions. A great deal can be said in the study of language without studying speech acts, but any such purely formal theory is necessarily incomplete.[13]

So far as *Speech Acts* is concerned, while many utterances happen to have semantic content, Searle is willing to include certain nonreferential utterances under the umbrella of "meaningful" so long as they are instrumental in producing certain effects on their audience—namely understanding. In that way, the early Searle is aligned with the communication-intention camp. However, as we will discuss in Chapter 7, with the publication of *Intentionality* (1983), Searle retreats from this position, ultimately aligning himself with the semanticists.

WHAT DISTINGUISHES SPEECH ACTS FROM OTHER KINDS OF ACTION? INTRODUCTION TO THE ILLOCUTIONARY INTENTIONS

What distinguishes speech acts from other kinds of (rational) action? Speech acts are meaningful, but what does Searle mean by meaningful? In the last section we considered two possibilities: according to the semanticist, speech acts are meaningful just in case they have truth conditions or conditions of satisfaction. This allows speech acts, unlike other actions such as boiling an egg, to represent the world as being a certain way. In *Speech Acts* Searle is sympathetic with, but ultimately rejects this criterion of meaning. While many speech acts do have conditions of satisfaction, certain speech acts, such as greetings, have no propositional content. In saying "hello," I am not modeling or representing the world under one aspect or another. I am just saying hello. This suggests a second conception of meaning: given the huge variety of speech acts, what property do they all share which accounts for our describing them as meaningful? In *Speech Acts* Searle endorses the communication-intention theorist's answer to that question. Speech acts are distinguished from other kinds of action in that they are made with the *intention to produce certain characteristic effects in the hearer*. This basic insight requires further elucidation.

All actions aim to produce some effect or other in the world. What is the characteristic effect that all speech acts aim to achieve, and which screen them off from other kinds of action? Searle formulates a modified version of Grice's answer to that question, quoted above: "In speaking I attempt to communicate certain things to my hearer by getting him to recognize my intention to communicate just those things."[14] While the significance of this claim may not yet be transparent, we can see that the speaker must have the following two intentions if his or her action is to further count as a speech act:

1. the intention to communicate—to produce a certain illocutionary effect in the hearer;
2. the intention to produce this effect by getting the hearer to recognize the intention to produce the effect;

To these, Searle also adds a third condition:

3. the intention to produce the effect by means of the hearer's knowledge of the rules governing the sentence.

For reasons discussed below, we will call these three Gricean conditions the *illocutionary intentions*. After briefly reviewing an objection to Searle's view, we will consider each of these three conditions in detail.

If the characteristic intended effect is to produce understanding in a hearer, what about soliloquy? Here, I appear to be speaking meaningfully, but I am not speaking with the intention of producing a communicative effect in a hearer because there are no hearers present. According to Searle's criteria, this action does not seem to qualify as a genuine speech act. In response to this objection, the early Searle follows Grice[15] in suggesting that soliloquy is a derivative, limiting case, where the speaker *is* the hearer. Thus, soliloquy can continue to count as meaningful so long as speakers intend to communicate with themselves.

THE FIRST ILLOCUTIONARY CONDITION OF A SPEECH ACT

All actions are body movements that result from ("because$_e$") intentional states. A condition that distinguishes speech acts from other kinds of action is that the speech acts involve the intention to produce understanding in a hearer. That is, to distinguish speech acts from other kinds of action, we have to survey the *contents* or conditions of satisfaction of the intentional states which cause the behavior.

Compare the action of boiling an egg with the speech act of saying "hello" to someone. Both actions are caused by a desire or some other intentional state with an upward, world-to-mind direction of fit. The condition of satisfaction of the chef's desire is that the egg be boiled; the chef's thought represents a possible world in which the egg is cooked. The condition of satisfaction of the speaker's desire is that the hearer comes to understand something. If the egg does not cook or the hearer fails to understand, the desire of the actor will be frustrated. But even if they failed to realize those conditions of satisfaction, they still would be said to have acted. To cook or speak or perform an action does not every time require that the actor *succeeds*. It only requires that their behavior is the result of a certain intention. But cooking and speaking differ precisely with respect to the *contents* of the intentional state which causes the behavior: in particular the chef is missing the intention to produce certain effects (understanding) in another person.

This, of course, is the essential intention by which Searle is identified as a communication-intention theorist. Something is meaningful, not because it represents the world, but because it was made with the intention of affecting the hearer.

What, exactly, is the nature of the intended effect that distinguishes speech acts from other kinds of acts? In brief, in speaking, the speaker intends to project the contents of some intentional state to the hearer.

Speech acts can be uttered with the intention of doing many things. In saying "hello," not only do I intend to communicate a greeting, but, depending on the context, I may be trying to endear myself to my interlocutors or distract or surprise or worry them. Which of these effects are operative in the speech act? Searle, following Austin, divides the many possible intended effects that may result from my speech into two broad categories: illocutionary effects and perlocutionary effects.

Consider the case where a customs agent orders a traveler to show a passport. There are at least two ways in which the order can *fail*. The traveler might understand the order but fail to produce the passport—perhaps it was forgotten or else the traveler becomes suddenly defiant. In this case the order fails to bring about the right sort of *perlocutionary effects*. The function of something is a certain intended consequence and the perlocutionary effects include those consequences; the reason or purpose as to why the official issued an order is to evoke some behavior or other in the hearer. But note that this kind of failure depends on the traveler's understanding the order in the first place; perlocutionary effects are the result of a set of *illocutionary effects*. Communication was *successful* in the sense that the traveler at least understood what was required. Given the understanding that the officer desires to see the passport, the traveler may decide to go ahead and comply with that order.

We have looked at a case where the officer's illocutionary intentions were successful (the utterance prompted the understanding or illocutionary effects in the hearer), but where the perlocutionary intentions were not successful (as when the traveler refused to show the passport in spite of understanding).

It may also be the case that the traveler is quite willing to hand over the passport, but the customs officer requests this in an unfamiliar language. That is, if the traveler does not know that "Könnte ich bitte den Pass sehen" *means* "I would like to see your passport" in German, the speech act is not successful. The order did not prompt understanding—the illocutionary effects in the hearer. Note that this is not the kind of failure which disqualifies the official's remark from counting as an order; it remains so, even though the hearer has not understood. It rather disqualifies the utterance from being a successful speech act in the sense of producing the right kind of illocutionary effects.

Understanding might be thought of as a kind of projection of a speaker's intentional contents from the speaker to the hearer, by way of some physical medium (sounds, scribbles, gestures). The officer has a desire that the traveler shows a passport. The projection is successful if the hearer comes to know about the officer's desire. But these illocutionary effects are produced with the ultimate *intention* of getting the hearer, not just to understand the order, but to show the passport. Thus the speaker's intended consequences are, first, that the traveler understand the officer's desire (the illocutionary effect) and, second, as a result, that the traveler shows the passport (the perlocutionary effect). We will discuss the notion of a perlocutionary effect and its associated speaker intentions below, in Chapters 6 and 7.

One difficulty is that the notions of *speech act*, *meaning*, *communication*, *understanding*, and *illocutionary effect* form a fairly tight logical circle. The contrast offered by the semanticist opens one way into this circle: if meaning something is not equivalent to referring to

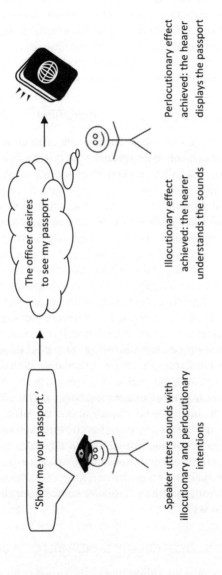

something, then it must involve an actor's attempt to communicate with a hearer. The fundamental unit of meaning is thus the speech act, wherein an agent intends to use physical sounds to produce a certain understanding or illocutionary effect in a hearer. Language then is not a two-part, timeless relation between word and object, but a temporal, multipart relation between two agents: the speaker's intentional store causes a word to be produced, which, if successful, projects a similar intentional state into the mind of the hearer.

THE SECOND ILLOCUTIONARY CONDITION OF A SPEECH ACT

There is a second condition which must be satisfied if an action is to qualify as a speech act. We have seen that it is necessary for an actor to intend to produce illocutionary effects in a hearer. This, however, is not a sufficient condition for speech. Searle, following Grice, also requires that the speaker must intend that the hearer recognizes that the speaker has the intention to produce understanding in the hearer.

Consider the following example, taken from Grice[16]: *one* kind of understanding a speaker might wish to induce in a hearer is a belief of some kind. Say that A wishes B to believe that C is a murderer. But the way that A does this is by surreptitiously leaving C's handkerchief at the site of the murder. This violates the second condition, in that, while A (the "speaker") intends to produce understanding in B (the "hearer"), A does not further intend that B recognize that A had this first intention. In this case, while the action might be successful (B now thinks C is the murderer), we are not tempted to think that in dropping the handkerchief A *meant* that C was the murderer. A's dropping the handkerchief is an action but does not count as a speech act.

In short, this intention, if its conditions of satisfaction are met, simply allows the hearer to know that the information gained was in fact intended to be communicated. It also, typically, allows the hearer to locate the source of the utterance. While this second condition might be regarded as a relatively minor qualification in comparison to the first condition, it has a broader significance that will become clearer in Chapter 6.

THE THIRD ILLOCUTIONARY CONDITION OF A SPEECH ACT

There is a final condition that must be satisfied if an action, further, is to count as a speech act. Not only must the hearer's understanding be among the speaker's conditions of satisfaction (the first condition), but the speaker must intend to bring about this understanding in a characteristic way. The third condition flags the *means* by which communication must happen if the act is to count as a genuine speech act: the speaker must act with the intention to produce understanding by *conventional* means. Conventionality implies an *arbitrary* association between sounds and their meaning. Searle writes,

> In the case of speech acts performed within a language . . . it is a matter of convention—as opposed to strategy, technique, procedure, or natural fact—that the utterance of such and such expressions under certain conditions counts as the making of a promise.[17]

In particular, a speaker must have an intention to produce understanding by means of the hearer's knowledge of the conventional, constitutive rules governing the use of the sentence.

Searle's appeal to the notion of a constitutive rule is a key feature of his account of speech acts. In Chapters 8 and 9 we will review his notion of a constitutive rule, as found in *The Construction of Social Reality*. For now, a few examples can illustrate Searle's requirement that speech has a conventional element.

Borrowing examples from Grice,[18] consider two ways in which Herod intends to impart understanding to Salome (so satisfying the first condition):

1. Herod presents to Salome John the Baptist's head on a platter.
2. Herod says to Salome, "John the Baptist is dead."

Similarly, compare:

1. Bill shows his bandaged leg, in response to an invitation to play squash.
2. Bill says "My leg is bandaged," in response to an invitation to play squash.

While Herod presented the head and Bill displayed his bandaged leg with the intention of producing understanding, it is not the case that in doing so they *meant* anything by what they did. However in uttering "John the Baptist is dead" or "My leg is bandaged," the action does have meaning; these utterances are speech acts.[19]

Given that both actors intend to induce understanding in another party, what is the difference between (1) and (2), such that only (2) appears to be a genuine case of meaning something? The fact that (2) is a verbalization is not relevant, as speech acts can have many physical bases, including sounds, marks, and gestures. The important difference, here, is that (2) is conventional: given the syntactic and semantic rules that help constitute the English language, the sounds "John the Baptist is dead" means that John the Baptist is dead. This conventionality is made evident by the fact that in another language, different combinations of sounds could have the same meaning, whereas the sounds "John the Baptist is dead" could mean something else entirely or else nothing at all. The head and bandaged leg are telling but are not conventional.

The requirement that the speaker intends to communicate *conventionally* concerns the *means* by which understanding is projected from speaker to hearer. The vehicle of communication must employ a set of constitutive rules or conventions that are agreed upon in advance by the interlocutors. In specifying what language is, Searle wants to screen out cases where some *natural* feature of the actor's behavior imparts understanding: smoke may indicate the presence of a fire or a plattered head may strongly indicate death, but the means by which these do so are natural and not conventional. A speaker acts with the intention of producing certain illocutionary and perlocutionary effects. In order for this action to count as a speech act, the action must somehow bring about those effects in a way that is not dependent on the physical features of the act alone. As we will see in Chapter 8, this third condition will be the basis for a more general distinction between institutional facts on the one hand and mere social facts on the other hand.

There are many cases that are on the cusp of meeting the third conventionality condition. We can intend to impart a belief that it is raining by saying (a) "It is raining" or (b) by pointing to a rain cloud. The first case clearly meets the conventionality requirement. But, is *pointing* sufficiently conventional? On the one hand, we seem hardwired to see this gesture as demonstrative. Bonobos and chimpanzees have been observed pointing in captivity. But, perhaps they learned this from their captors (there has been only one anecdotal report of a bonobo pointing in the wild).[20] And even if it is hardwired, would the gesture then not count as conventional? After all, a pointing gesture does not *physically compel* us to trace a pointing gesture from hand to finger tip to object. And if pointing seems clear, what about the case where an actor pokes another or else imitates the sound of a predator in order to alert companions? [21] Searle is not obligated to so precisely delimit the sphere of the conventional: indeed, the very ability to appreciate the way in which these cases are borderline presupposes sufficient competence to understand the third conventionality requirement.

In Chapter 8, we will consider more pressing difficulties with the requirement that language (or any other institutional fact) must perform its function by conventional means—a means that is not entirely dependent on the physical structure of the action.

SEARLE'S GRICEAN MODEL OF ILLOCUTIONARY ACTS: SUMMARY

In this chapter we have reviewed the three criteria by which we might distinguish speech acts from other kinds of action. In general a speech action, unlike other actions, must be caused by intentional states with three characteristic contents: first, the speaker must intend to communicate with the hearer. This is equivalent to the requirement that a speaker must intend to prompt understanding or illocutionary effects in the hearer. In communicating, a speaker projects a certain intentional content into the head of the hearer by certain means (gestures, sounds, marks). According to the second condition, the speaker must intend that the hearer recognizes that the speaker has the first intention. If the first two illocutionary intentions are to be satisfied, the hearer will acquire the desired understanding and also understand that the speaker intended the hearer to acquire it. The second intention, among other things, allows the hearer to locate the source of the understanding. The third requirement places a condition on the *means* by which communication must happen. In projecting an intentional state from the speaker to the hearer, it must happen over a medium that is conventional. Speech does not just happen by way of, for example, sound, but those sounds must be given significance by a community of language users: thus, crying or wailing are, at best, outlier cases of meaning.

We can represent the difference between speech acts and other kinds of action as follows in Figure 5.2.

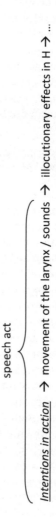

action

intentions in action → body movement

speech act

Intentions in action → movement of the larynx / sounds → illocutionary effects in H → …

Intentions in action must include the three illocutionary intentions:

(1) intention to communicate with, or produce illocutionary effects in the hearer

(2) intention that the hearer knows the speaker's intention (1)

(3) intention to communicate with hearer by conventional means (sounds, gestures, etc.)

CHAPTER 6

FROM SOUNDS TO WORDS:
THE INTENTION TO REPRESENT

In this chapter we will expand the basic account of a speech act. The basic account holds that an action is a speech act if the behavior or sound is caused by the illocutionary intentions: the intention to communicate and the intention that the hearer recognizes the speaker's intention to communicate. In particular, communication involves the speaker's intention to produce illocutionary effects in the hearer. Furthermore, the speaker must intend to communicate by conventional means.

There are two points at which we need to extend this basic account of linguistic behavior. First, a speaker's illocutionary intentions are *preceded* by a set of preliminary intentions: the speaker's intentional object of communication and a speaker's perlocutionary intentions. The object of communication—what Searle calls the "sincerity condition"—is the intentional state which the speaker wishes to project to the hearer. The perlocutionary intention includes the function or purpose of the speech act (so far as the hearer's behavior is concerned). Second, *after* the agent's illocutionary intentions, but before the actual utterance, the speaker must exercise the *intention to represent*, which makes it possible for a sound to be a conventional vehicle of communication.

These two additions can be mapped on to the basic account of speech acts as shown in Figure 6.1.

AUSTIN AND SEARLE ON SPEECH ACTS

Part of the technical accomplishment of *Speech Acts* lies in the fact that Searle synthesizes the views of two of the communication-intention

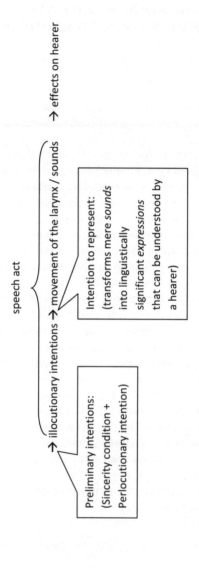

tradition's founding fathers: Paul Grice and John Austin. Chapter 5 articulated Searle's account of a speech act under its Gricean aspect: speech acts are differentiated from other kinds of action in that speech acts are undertaken by way of characteristic intentions, including the intention to produce understanding in the hearer. But in describing these Gricean intentions as "illocutionary"— Austin's word—Searle makes the novel and interesting suggestion that these intentions can be *embedded* into Austin's overall account of linguistic behavior.

In saying something, Austin suggests that we are actually engaged in three distinguishable acts: locutionary, illocutionary, and perlocutionary acts.

The illocutionary act includes, according to Searle's interpretation of Austin, the three Gricean intentions to communicate. If successful, it culminates in the hearer's understanding that the speaker has some intention or other (e.g. the traveler understands that the officer wants to see the passport).[1]

The locutionary act involves the intention to make sounds and words which should lead to the hearer's understanding. Austin subdivides the locutionary act into three constitutive acts. At base is the phonetic act, which he describes as "the act of uttering certain noises."[2] Above that is the phatic act, which he characterizes as "the uttering of certain vocables or words, i.e. noises of certain types, belonging to and as belonging to, a certain vocabulary, conforming to and as conforming to a certain grammar."[3] Finally the rhetic act is "an act of using those vocables with a certain more-or-less definite sense and reference."[4] Austin's locutionary intentions include two of the three intentions needed to transform sounds to words, as required by Searle (discussed below).

A speaker performs the locutionary and illocutionary act with the intention of securing illocutionary uptake, so that the hearer comes to understand what the speaker said. An illocutionary act is "happily" performed if such uptake is secured. Searle glosses Austin's notion of happiness in terms of the fulfillment of the conditions of satisfaction which underlie each of the various acts.

In addition to understanding (the illocutionary effect), there are, as we have seen, further effects a speaker may or may not achieve in performing a speech act. Recall the passport example in Chapter 5: if a customs official orders a traveler to produce a passport, the speech act will be illocutionarily happy if the traveler understands what is demanded. Illocutionary failure might happen if the request is made in a language not understood by the traveler. The utterance is also made with certain perlocutionary effects in mind—namely that the hearer comes to actually show the passport. Thus, the utterance may be illocutionarily successful but perlocutionarily unsuccessful if the hearer forgot the passport or else became suddenly defiant.

Austin's overall account of saying something can be represented as shown in Figure 6.2, on the next page.

The illocutionary intention, according to Searle's reading of Austin,[5] consists of the intention to communicate plus the other two Gricean intentions discussed in Chapter 5.

But why communicate? The causal chain typically *starts* with the perlocutionary intention, which is what motivates or provides a functional basis for the speech act. The officer made the noises "show your passport"—the phonetic/locutionary effect—in order that he satisfies his illocutionary intention to communicate with the traveler. But the overall *point* of communicating is not simply to get the traveler to understand the order, but to get the traveler to show the passport (the perlocutionary effect). The speaker represents this purpose by way of the perlocutionary intention.

In a recent essay on speech acts, Kent Bach offers a comparison by which to orient the reader to the significance of Austin's constellation of intentions, acts, and their associated effects:

> The illocutionary act is but *one level of the total speech act* that one performs in uttering a sentence. Consider that in general when one acts intentionally, one has *a set of nested intentions*. For instance, having arrived home without your keys, you might move your finger in a certain way with the intention not just of moving your finger in that way but with further intentions of pushing a certain button, ringing the doorbell, arousing your spouse . . . and ultimately getting into your house. The single bodily movement in moving your finger *comprises of a multiplicity of actions*, each corresponding to a different one of the nested intentions. Similarly, speech acts are not just acts of producing certain sounds.[6]

Bach brings Austin's distinction under a familiar and commonsensical picture—actions are conglomerate, consisting of various, nested intentions. He wants to understand the illocutionary act according to

SPEAKER

The performance of a speech act involves the following three acts, each of which are underlain by characteristic intention (e.g., illocutionary intentions):

3. Locutionary intentions/acts
2. Illocutionary intentions/acts
1. Perlocutionary intention/act

HEARER

These acts are 'happy' if they produce characteristic effects in the hearer. In Searle's terms, these effects are the intention's conditions of satisfaction:

4. Locutionary effect (sound)
5. Illocutionary effect (understanding)
6. Perlocutionary effect (function)

Perlocutionary effect

phonetic effect

Phonetic intention/act

(book metaphor)

Perlocutionary intention/act

a model of nested intentions, so that alerting my spouse is causally dependent on the act of pressing the doorbell which is, in turn, dependent on my intentions to do both.

This way of framing Austin, which Searle endorses, has some characteristic consequences: the nested pattern of intentions might, as indicated in the figure above, be thought of as an open book. The open pages are the locutionary (phonetic) intention and the locutionary (phonetic) effect. The fact that these two pages are adjacent represents causal immediacy: the intention to make sounds immediately causes the sounds to be made. Pushing the metaphor further, the front and back cover correspond to the perlocutionary intention and its conditions of satisfaction, the perlocutionary effect. Unlike the phonetic intention, it will be noticed that in speech these are not causally adjacent. A perlocutionary intention can only be satisfied *if* the speaker then forms illocutionary and locutionary intentions. The illocutionary and locutionary intentions and their effects are all *means* by which the perlocutionary function is fulfilled. If those intentions' conditions of satisfaction are then satisfied, then the perlocutionary intention might also be satisfied. The perlocutionary intention is vitally important to understanding the significance of the overall act: it typically provides the motivation or function, which explains why a speaker is making a noise in the first place.

The book metaphor holds up remarkably well in capturing the corresponding features of Bach's example. The front cover is the functional intention of the act: the intention to get in your house. The back cover is the realization of that intention. But, given that you do not have keys, in order to satisfy that intention you must intend to perform a number of ancillary acts: the intention to alert your wife, the intention to ring the door bell, and so on. These constitute the means by which you can get into the house. At one point there is an intention whose conditions of satisfaction do not require that you intend a further means. There must be some intention that is causally adjacent to its conditions of satisfaction: the intention to move your finger directly precipitates the finger movement. This intention-effect pair are the open pages. Once the finger moves, a causal chain is set in motion which, if nothing goes wrong, will eventuate in the satisfaction of the desire to get in the house, which is the point of ringing the doorbell.

Notice that in this example, it is always possible to move your finger with the intention of getting in your house, while it is not, at least in some circumstances, possible to get in your house without moving your finger. Nevertheless, while the finger movement might be perceived as having a kind of causal autonomy that the other actions in the sequence do not have (it is not dependent on any other action), it is also important to see that its significance or justification *depends* on that initial desire to get in the house. That is, if pushing the doorbell is not ontologically or causally dependent on the first functional intention, it is nevertheless only justified given that latter intention. This functional asymmetry, between efficient causation and functional justification, will be the basis of a criticism of Searle's account of speech acts offered in Chapter 7.

Having already discussed the illocutionary level of intentions in the last chapter, we will now explicate the perlocutionary intentions that proceed and the locutionary intentions that follow those illocutionary intentions.

PERLOCUTIONARY INTENTIONS AND
THE SINCERITY CONDITION

Perlocutionary intentions include, as their conditions of satisfaction, desired effects on the hearer that follow those effects prompted by the illocutionary intention. As noted, the point or function of the utterance, so far as the hearer is concerned, is typically found within these perlocutionary intentions. The officer's illocutionary intentions are satisfied if the traveler understands the sounds "show your passport" to have the same force and content as the officer's desire that the traveler show the passport. But the ultimate point or function of the order is to have the traveler, not just to understand the illocutionary act, but to show the passport.[7]

Can a perlocutionary intention be satisfied through nonillocutionary means? Yes and no. Of course, sometimes the perlocutionary intention can be satisfied though noncommunicative means, as when the passport official forcibly takes the traveler's passport. But there are weak and strong senses in which a perlocutionary intention *cannot* be satisfied by nonillocutionary means. The weak sense: there are some functional, perlocutionary intentions that require an illocutionary intention—if I am playing blackjack, and I want the dealer to deal me another card, I could not satisfy that intention without the illocutionary act culminating with the sound "hit." For example, if I physically strong-armed the dealer to give me a card, this does not count as being *dealt* a card; in exercising these alternative means of satisfying my perlocutionary intention, I have altogether ceased to play Blackjack. So, some perlocutionary effects appear to require illocutionary means. Likewise, while I might be able to produce the understanding that I'm about to do something through nonlinguistic means (I raise the hammer over the nail), I cannot produce in someone the understanding that I have *promised* to do something through nonlinguistic means. The strong sense in which a perlocutionary intention requires an illocutionary intention banks on a grammatical point: perlocutionary literally means "around-locutionary," so that the identification of an intention of an effect as *perlocutionary* entails that the effect is brought about by way of a communicative act.

Not all perlocutionary intentions are functional, activity-defining intentions. For example, in addition to wanting the traveler to display the passport, the officer may also want to intimidate the traveler. This intention is not an illocutionary intention but may nevertheless require an illocutionary intention to be satisfied. In ordering the traveler to display the passport, the officer thus prompts two perlocutionary effects in addition to understanding: the displaying of the passport and the feeling of fear and intimidation in the traveler. But the *point* of his asking—the one which justifies the speech act—is only found in the first perlocutionary effect.

There can also be a broader class of perlocutionary effects that are not even intended by the speaker. The notion of perlocutionary effect flags *any* effect on the hearer that is brought about in virtue of their understanding the speaker's utterance. If the official's request inadvertently causes the traveler to be late, that is among the perlocutionary effects of the speech act.

We might thus distinguish between three classes of perlocutionary effects: there are (1) the primary, functional, and intended consequences (the hearer shows the passport), there are (2) the other intended consequences (the hearer feels intimidated), and there are (3) the unintended consequences (the hearer is made late). The second category might further be subdivided into (2a) those intended consequences that are a means to the primary consequences and (2b) those that are not. Depending on the context, the officer's intention to intimidate could be construed as either of these.

Unless otherwise noted, we will use "perlocutionary intentions" and "perlocutionary effects" to flag the first class—the primary purposive intentions and their effects.

In spite of the importance certain perlocutionary intentions play in rationalizing or justifying the illocutionary and locutionary acts, these intentions have been downplayed by most communication-intention theorists, including Searle and Austin. Exceptions include Grice,[8] Stephen Shiffer,[9] and Robert Stalnaker.[10]

Before we can understand Searle's account of the intention to represent, something else must be in place before a speaker forms an illocutionary intention: In order to intend to communicate there *must be something to say*—some intentional state that the speaker wants to put into the head of the hearer. This intentional state, which Searle calls the "sincerity condition," is the object of communication or transmission.

Sometimes the sincerity condition is identical with the functional, perlocutionary intention: the officer's desire that the traveler show a passport *is* precisely the intention the speaker wishes to project to the traveler. It may not be that the officer *says* "I desire to see your passport," but whatever is said—"please show your passport"—has exactly the same conditions of satisfaction as the intention flagged by the sincerity condition. A number of factors influence *how* exactly these conditions of satisfaction are expressed, including the need to imply the presence of preparatory conditions, such as appropriate institutional structures, as well as certain prudential considerations including professionalism, etiquette, and so on. Note that the perlocutionary intention/sincerity condition is, in this case, different from the communication intention.

Sometimes the sincerity condition is closely connected to, but distinguishable from, the functional perlocutionary intention: for example, a speaker may desire that *the hearer believes that it is raining outside*. This intention will be satisfied if this friend comes to believe that this is the case. However, according to Searle, the sincerity condition—the intentional state which I communicate—is only: *the speaker believes it is raining outside (I believe it is raining outside)*. The communication intention is successful if the hearer comes to believe that the speaker believes that it is raining outside. But there remains an additional step until the speaker's perlocutionary intention is satisfied: the hearer *may* take the fact that the speaker believes that it is raining outside to be a reason to likewise believe it. Once the hearer believes that it is raining, which is different than believing that the speaker believes it to be raining (the sincerity condition), the speaker's perlocutionary intention is satisfied.

The fact that we can distinguish the functional perlocutionary intention from the sincerity condition is the basis by which Searle famously criticizes Grice's account of meaning. This criticism also motivates Searle's modified version of Grice's account of meaning as presented in Chapter 5. Where Searle focuses on the illocutionary effect, Grice emphasizes the perlocutionary, functional effect. In Chapter 7, we will see that Searle's criticism of Grice also provides the rationale for a further revision of Searle's account of meaning, as found in *Intentionality* and in "Meaning, Communication and Representation."

Both the author of *Speech Acts* and Grice agree that meaning must be construed in terms of the intention to communicate; a sound or action counts as meaningful if it is made with the intention to produce certain effects in the hearer, plus the other illocutionary intentions. But which effects? Looking at a typical case of assertion, the speaker must have two intentional states before forming the intention to communicate. First, the speaker *believes* p (say, that it is raining outside) and, second, the speaker *desires* that the hearer should also believe that p. Simply believing something is not sufficient to prompt the intention to communicate. Every action, as we have seen in Chapter 4, requires a motivator. A typical motivator for expressing a belief is that the hearer does not know or is mistaken about the climatic conditions. This motivator has, as its conditions of satisfaction, the purpose or function of the communication; the desire that the hearer believes that it is raining.

The speaker's belief that it is raining is the object of communication—the sincerity condition. The perlocutionary intention (motivator) and the sincerity condition jointly give rise to the *desire* or intention to communicate, the first of the illocutionary intentions. This illocutionary intention to communicate is a means by which the perlocutionary intention might be satisfied.

Given this, Searle's criticism of Grice's account of meaning is relatively simple. Grice appears to require that in order to mean something the speaker must intend that the hearer believe that it is raining (desire 1). When we assert p, we aim to *convince* the hearer that, in fact, p. Searle objects to this. While we often assert p with the perlocutionary aim of convincing the hearer that p, this is not necessary in order to mean something. Meaning something only requires that the speaker attempts to communicate p to the hearer. And this is possible even if the speaker does not further intend that the hearer

Belief: it is raining (sincerity condition)

Desire 2: communicate belief to hearer (illocutionary intention) ——→

Desire 1: that hearer believe that it is raining (perlocutionary, functional intention) believes or is convinced of it. A perlocutionary intention—at least not the perlocutionary intention to convince (desire 1)—is not a necessary ingredient of a speaker's meaning something. To communicate, the speaker only needs a desire to communicate (desire 2), which is possible without desire 1.

Along these lines, Searle criticizes Grice's inclusion of perlocutionary intentions as among the three illocutionary-meaning-communication intentions:

[E]ven where there generally is a correlated perlocutionary effect, I may say something and mean it without in fact intending to produce that effect. Thus, for example, I may make a statement without caring whether my audience believes it or not but simply because I feel it my duty to make it.[11]

We will return to Searle's criticism of Grice in the next chapter. For now, it is worth considering whether in saying something out of duty, I do not, in fact, have the perlocutionary intention to convince the audience of what I am saying. Not having the *expectation* that the perlocutionary intention will be satisfied is not the same as not having a perlocutionary intention.[12] Perhaps people pray with the expectation that their prayers will not be answered or heard; but that is not tantamount to the fact that their prayer was, thus, not a supplication. Perhaps Grice recognizes that there is a sense in which we do not *mean* what we say unless the speaker, further, thinks that a hearer ought to believe it.

FROM SOUNDS TO WORDS: THE BRIDGE FROM THE SPEAKER'S ILLOCUTIONARY INTENTION TO THE HEARER'S UNDERSTANDING

Looking at assertion, a speaker begins with the following intentional states: the speaker believes something, p, and the speaker desires that the hearer believe p. This is the speaker's sincerity condition and functional perlocutionary intention, respectively. The illocutionary or speech act begins with the intention to communicate to a hearer that the speaker believes p. To this is added the two other illocutionary intentions: the intention that the hearer recognizes that the speaker has the previous intention and the intention that the communication happens by conventional means.

We now need to explain *how* the sincerity condition can be communicated conventionally. Searle construes this conventional component of speech as a kind of bridge that links the speaker's three illocutionary intentions with each of their conditions of satisfaction. The third illocutionary intention is satisfied if a sound or gesture comes to represent the same conditions of satisfaction that are found in the sincerity condition (p). The second illocutionary intention is satisfied when the hearer recognizes that the speaker intended the sound to represent the fact that the speaker believes p. Combining the third and second condition, the hearer comes to understand that *the speaker believes p*: "I achieve the intended effect on the hearer by getting him to recognize my intention to achieve that effect, and as soon as the hearer recognizes what it is my intention to achieve, it is in general achieved."[13] With the satisfaction of the three illocutionary intentions' conditions of satisfaction, the speaker has achieved the desired illocutionary effect: the hearer now understands that the speaker believes p. But the speaker's perlocutionary intention has not been satisfied until the hearer further comes to believe, not just that the speaker believes p, but p itself. Typically, but not always, the fact that a hearer believes that the speaker believes p is sufficient reason for the hearer to believe p. At that moment, the speaker's perlocutionary intention is satisfied.

The task is to build the center span of the illocutionary bridge. The bridge begins with the speaker's intention to communicate a belief that p (the sincerity condition) by conventional means. The bridge ends with a sound or action that the hearer can recognize as an expression, the contents which match that of the sincerity condition.

We have seen in Chapter 3 that intentional states have conditions of satisfaction brought under one psychological mode or another. In this case, the condition of satisfaction is p and the psychological mode is belief, which has a downward direction of fit. The question, then, is how can *sounds* have these properties—properties of mind. Sounds can be loud, soft, high, low, and shrill. But how can they further represent the world as being a certain way (p), with a downward direction of fit? Superficially, it seems that someone who ascribes such intentional properties to noises is making a category mistake, as when someone ascribes anger to a storm cloud or design to a banana. How is it possible that mere noises can be the bearer of intentional properties? And why do they have these properties? Just as an intentional state has both representational content and psychological force, words likewise have propositional content and illocutionary force.

Searle does not think that the parallel between our mental states and our words is simply a happy accident. Rather, the intentional structure of our words mirrors that of intentional states because the intentional states *explain* the structure of our linguistic utterances. Without a substructure of intentionality, words are simply sounds, marks, or gestures. Intentionality, at least in human beings, has the unique and extraordinary power to impart its own structure on otherwise dead or lifeless phenomena. Words, then, have what Searle calls "derived intentionality."

I may believe that Valentina Tereshkova was the first woman in space quite independent of my saying so. This is a psychological event that takes place within a private sphere of consciousness. This intentional state has representative content that represents a possible world in which Valentina Tereshkova was the first woman in space. Moreover, the intentional force is such that the content is cast as having a downward, mind-to-world direction of fit: it is a belief, not a desire. In this case the represented possible world is isomorphic with the actual world, so that the belief is in fact *true*. If Valentina Tereshkova was not, in fact, the first woman in space, I would be obligated to change my belief. For intentional states with a downward direction of fit, such as belief, in case of a mis-fit between content (W_p) and world (W_a), I am obliged to change the content.

Sounds and marks become meaningful when I project an intentional state's force and content onto objects and events in the world, so that the publicly available sounds and marks can come to represent Valentina Tereshkova as being the first woman in space. In English the sounds "Valentina Tereshkova was the first woman in space" have come to mean simply that this woman was the first woman to fly outside the earth's atmosphere. It has the same force and content as the corresponding belief (which is, further, its sincerity condition). I could likewise impose the same intentional content on the nonsense sound "gremple" or, for that matter, a glass of water, but because this imposition is private or idiosyncratic my doing so more or less guarantees that my illocutionary and perlocutionary intentions will go unsatisfied. For Searle, unlike Wittgenstein, a private language is not incoherent or impossible, but imprudent.

How does intentionality impose its own structure—content and force—onto sounds and marks? An assertion, in which sounds or marks represent Valentina Tereshkova as being the first woman in space, consists of three[14] basic intentions:[15]

1. *The belief that Valentina Tereshkova was the first woman in space.* The content of this intention represents a possible world in which Valentina Tereshkova was the first woman in space (a possible world which happens in fact to correspond to the actual world) and has a force with a downward, mind-to-world direction of fit. This is the sincerity condition.[16]

2. *A desire that the belief in (1) causes me to utter the noises "Valentina Tereshkova was the first woman in space"* (or "gremple," or whatnot). This is simply a desire to make some sound, mark, or gesture which will come to mean something. The intentional content of this second intention includes the sounds themselves. But this intention has an upward, world-to-mind direction of fit, the conditions of satisfaction are only satisfied when the world is changed to match this content. I then satisfy those conditions by making the noises. Austin calls this the "phonetic intention," a kind of locutionary intention.

This second intention is what Austin calls the locutionary-phonetic intention and is satisfied when the sound is made. Note that this phonetic intention and its conditions of satisfaction are causally adjacent, as represented by the open pages of the book of nested intentions and effects. Note that intention (1) does cause intention (2) but they are not causally adjacent. The sincerity condition causes the three illocutionary intentions which then cause the locutionary-phonetic intention.

3. *A desire to impose the first intention's content and force on the sounds that result from the second intention—"Valentina Tereshkova was the first woman in space."* This third intention imbues those sounds with a kind of derived intentionality that mirrors the structure of the sincerity condition. Searle calls this third intention, "the intention to represent"[17] or else the "essential condition."[18] Austin calls this the locutionary-rhetic intention.[19]

Note that Searle seems to suggest that the intention to communicate *follows* the locutionary-phonetic intention, whereas Austin appears to reverse the order of causation. Against Searle it seems strange that I first make a noise and then impose a force and content on it, as if there is a moment when the noise is just a noise. Austin's view captures the sense in which the words we speak are always already meaningful. It should be noted, however, that at this level of discussion, neither Searle nor Austin seem overly committed to a precise temporal sequencing of the required intentions.

Communication is now possible. Because the speaker imposed a force and content on the brute phenomena which is both conventional and public, the hearer is now in a position to interpret the sound. The first illocutionary effect of the utterance is that the hearer believes that the sound conventionally means *Valentina Tereshkova was the first woman in space* (satisfying the third illocutionary intention). This leads to another illocutionary effect, wherein the hearer ascribes that belief to the speaker (satisfying the second illocutionary intention), and so comes to believe that *the speaker believes that Valentina Tereshkova was the first woman in space* (satisfying the first illocutionary intention). Finally, all things being equal, the hearer's belief that *the speaker believes Valentina Tereshkova was the first woman in space* provides a reason for the hearer to think that, indeed, *Valentina Tereshkova is the first woman in space*. This is a perlocutionary effect. If the speaker's functional, perlocutionary intention is to convince the hearer of this fact (and not just convince the hearer that the speaker believes this to be the case), then it will also have been satisfied.

Extending Hubert Dreyfus's criticism of Searle's account of action, he might criticize Searle's account of meaning something on the following grounds: according to Searle, the speaker will have formulated seven different intentions in order to make a simple assertion. But, in surveying our own phenomenology in speaking, it does not *feel* as though we had all of these intentions: we just spoke.[20] Grice articulates a similar concern when he "disclaim[s]" the "peopling of our talking life with armies of complicated psychological occurrences."[21] Searle responds to Dreyfus's criticism, somewhat obscurely, by contending that in providing this analysis he is not doing phenomenology but "logical analysis."[22]

The speech act that we have considered is an assertion, wherein a speaker attempts to describe or characterize the world as being a certain way. The intention which underlies statements (its sincerity condition) is a belief. But statements or assertions are only one kind of speech act: we can, for example, make promises, orders, requests, show appreciation, criticize, apologize, censure, approve, argue, welcome, warn, and make declarations. Each of these speech acts share

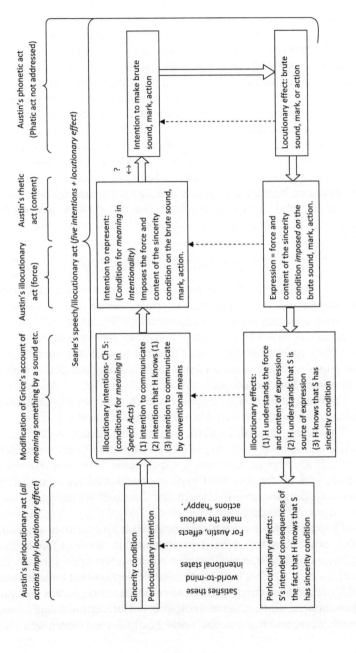

the same intentional structure in that there is an underlying intention or sincerity condition which is projected to the hearer by conventional means. This condition must be causally connected to the utterance and there is an intention which gives the utterance the same conditions of satisfaction as is found in the sincerity condition. For example, I promise to do something if (1) I intend to do x, (2) that intention causes me to make certain sounds, and (3) those sounds— "I promise to do x"—put the speaker under the obligation to do x. I may, further, communicate my promise to a hearer when I say "I promise to do x" with the intention that the hearer understands that these sounds have the specified conditions of satisfaction.

While each type of speech act will be underlain by a distinct kind of intention, Searle recommends that all speech acts fall under one of five distinct families. In the next section we will review Searle's taxonomy of speech acts.

A TAXONOMY OF SPEECH ACTS

In the previous section we looked at the speech act, "Valentina Tereshkova was the first woman in space." Searle calls this class of speech acts *assertives*. We make assertions when we wish to make a claim about how a part of the world is. In other words, assertives are truth functional and have the condition of satisfaction that there exists a state of affairs that corresponds with that which is represented by the assertion.

There are four other classes of speech acts, besides assertives: directives, commissives, expressives, and declarations.[23]

If assertives have a downward, word-to-world direction of fit, both directives and commissives have an upward, world-to-word direction of fit. That is, for an assertion, a mis-fit between the possible world represented by the assertion and the world itself is corrected by changing the assertion. If I assert that the closet is empty and I say that it is full, the fault lies with what I say—the speech act is what needs to be changed to rectify the misfit. But for directives and commissives, if there is a mismatch between that which is represented by the words and the way that the world is, the fault lies with the world; I need to fill my closet. In spite of the fact that the sentences look somewhat different, a directive—"Fill the closet"—has the same propositional content as an assertive, "The closet is full." Both sentences represent a possible world in which the closet is full. The syntactical difference between the two speech acts is explained by the fact that they have two different directions of fit. If in the actual world the closet is in fact empty, because "fill the closet" has a world-to-word direction of fit, this speech act is satisfied not by changing the propositional content, but by changing the world.

Directives are denoted by verbs such as *ask, order, command, request, beg, plead, pray,* and *entreat.* If there is a misalignment between the speaker's propositional content and the way that the world in fact is, a directive will be successful if the hearer changes the world so that it matches the content. Because directives have an upward, world-to-word direction of fit, they must be founded on a speaker's intention which likewise has a world-to-mind direction of fit such as wanting, wishing, or desiring. This underlying intention is the directive's sincerity condition.

Commissives commit the speaker to a future course of action as when a promise is made. If directives are distinguished from assertives in terms of direction of fit, why have an additional class of speech acts—commissives—which share a directive's world-to-word direction of fit? After all, both directives and commissives are satisfied when the world is changed to be in accordance with some propositional content. What is the difference between saying "empty the closet," a directive, and "I promise to empty the closet," a commissive? Why not combine both kinds of speech act into one super category? A request or order—a directive—tries to get the *hearer* to do something (change the world to line up with the speech act's propositional content) whereas a promise—a commissive—commits the *speaker* to do something. This difference in who is supposed to evoke the change is pronounced enough to justify cleaving these kinds of acts in two, in spite of the fact that they have the same direction of fit.

Sometimes the point of our utterance is neither to say something about how the world is (assertive) nor to express an intention to have it changed in some way (directive/commissive). We feel grateful, apologetic, or else find ourselves loathing or admiring things. These feelings almost always have a propositional content that frames or explains the feeling. I normally do not just have vague and undirected feelings of gratitude. When feeling this way, I am grateful because of the fact that, for example, someone watched my cat while I was away, I'm happy because I passed the test, or else I deplore someone for exploiting a helpless stranger. While the feeling is a nonintentional state, it is typically framed by some set of intentional contents; the

Speech acts	Direction of fit	Sincerity condition: psychological state expressed
Assertives: ⊢	→	Belief: B(p)
Directives: !	←	Want, wish, desire: W(H does A)
Commissives: C	←	Intention: I(S does A)
Expressives: E	∅	Some psychological state of the speaker/hearer
Declarations: D	↔	∅ (none)

feeling or attitude is about something. *Expressives,* a fourth category of speech acts in Searle's taxonomy, are performed when we articulate feelings: "Thank you for watching my cat" or "It's disgusting the way you exploited that person."

Expressives have no direction of fit. There may be some tendency to think that we are reporting or describing some (internal) state of affairs *qua* an assertive. But Searle is right not to collapse or paraphrase the expression "Thank you" into the assertion "I am (in fact) feeling gratitude." We are not, in the latter case, making a truth claim about how the world in fact is. Searle claims that the truth of the assertion that I'm feeling gratitude is presupposed and not put up for evaluation, as in the case when I assert that the fuel tank is full. Moreover, I'm not trying to change any feature of the world; "Thank you" requires no course of action on the part of a speaker or hearer. It is simply the external expression of what is at base some feeling. Typically when I say, "It's disgusting the way you exploited that person," I also imply the directive "don't exploit people," whose conditions of satisfaction are satisfied when the hearer ceases to take advantage of people. But it is not necessary to imply this much, so that I might express my disgust just to express my disgust; perhaps, I know that the person cannot or will not change and so do not bother to further intend that they do. Expressives amplify or put into the public sphere nonintentional states; they do not, unlike assertives, directives, or commissives, have conditions of satisfaction. so, they do not have a direction of fit.

A final class of speech act is the *declaration.* If expressives are distinguished from the first three types of speech act by not having a direction of fit, declarations are marked by having *both* a word-to-world *and* a world-to-word direction of fit.

In special circumstances we can bring facts into existence simply by declaring that it exists. If God's saying, "Let there be light," is sufficient to bring about light, this is a declaration. Obviously humans cannot will brute facts into existence, so that my lawn is not mowed simply by virtue of my saying that it is so. But there is a class of facts that are in some sense created by us—what Searle calls institutional facts. For example, the Queen can dub or declare that a man is a knight. Just by virtue of her saying so, the man becomes a knight. This is a curious function of language, which, as we will see, occupies a central place in accounting for the possibility of speech acts in particular and institutional facts in general.

Almost all linguistic acts have a representational component and so involve an attempt to get the world and our words to match. In the event of a mis-fit, assertives, directives, and commissives provoke us to change either the words or the world so as to bring them into alignment. This is a sense in which language is inherently normative; words, themselves, imply robust deontological commitments. Declarations—when certain conditions are met—bring the world in alignment to the words *simply by virtue of their being said*. Where an assertive has a word-to-world direction of fit and directives and commissives have a world-to-word direction of fit, directives have both a word-to-world and world-to-word direction of fit. As such the directive can be expected to share certain illocutionary properties with assertives, directives, and commissives while remaining importantly distinct from these speech acts. Directives are not assertives, which aim to describe the world as being a certain way. When someone declares "the meeting is adjourned," they are not reporting or stating an antecedently existing fact; their saying it makes it so. Nevertheless the declaration resembles an assertion in the sense that the utterance is true, which is why both a declaration and an assertion share a word-to-world direction of fit. A declaration also has a world-to-word direction of fit, like a directive or a commissive. It is like a commissive or directive in the sense that a speaker says something with the intention of bringing about some change in the world—the meeting is to be closed or the man becomes a knight. But unlike commissives or directives there is, when said under the right circumstances, no gap between the speaker's declaring something and it becoming the case. However, when I promise or ask someone to mow my lawn, my commissive or directive is not sufficient to make it so.

Note that a number of conditions need to be in place before, "The meeting is adjourned," "I pronounce you man and wife," and "I dub thee knight" count as declarations. There has to be an institution wherein something counts as a meeting, a marriage, or a knight. Moreover, the person making the declaration must have a special status within that institution: typically only certain people within that institution are enabled to adjourn a meeting, consecrate a marriage, or dub a knight. Those people must exercise the declaration properly as dictated by convention. Depending on how highly codified the rules are, a chairperson's saying, "Let's call it a day," might not count as an adjourning. Finally, that person has to *intend* that the utterance counts as a declaration. If a chairperson was reading a transcript of a previous meeting and so happened to say the words, "The meeting is adjourned," that would not count as an adjourning: it lacks the requisite intention. Similarly, a living will made under duress—and so not intended—would not normally count as a binding contract.

While declaratives are distinguishable from the other speech acts in having two directions of fit, there is a way in which other speech acts can be embedded *within* a declarative speech act. Searle calls these linguistic declarations "performatives".[24] That is, there are two ways to perform a speech act: on the one hand we can do it, so that if it is raining I might just say "It is raining." On the other hand I might opt to embed a verb which makes explicit the statement's illocutionary force: "I assert that it is raining." Where both these speech acts make a claim about the state of the weather (an assertive), the latter embeds the assertive into a declarative: to say that "I'm asserting p" is sufficient to make it an assertion. Note that the declarative aspect does not extend to the content of the assertion: to say that I'm asserting that it is raining is not sufficient to make it rain; it only makes it the case that p is an assertion. Similarly, I can say either, "Wash the car!" or "I'm ordering you to wash the car!" While both are directives (orders), the latter is also a declarative: whatever content follows "I'm ordering you . . . " is an order simply by virtue of my having said that it is so. Both these linguistic declarations, such as "I assert that . . . ," and extralinguistic declarations, such as a queen who says "I dub thee knight," have two directions of fit: saying that the noises are an assertion or that the person is a knight makes it so.

Why can every speech act be rearticulated, without a change in content, in a way that makes reference to a declaration (performative)? In the last section we saw that every speech act involves the intention to represent. This is simply the intention to transform sounds into meaningful artifacts. This cognitive capacity can be explicitly articulated. Just as a queen can dub a man a knight, we can dub a sound to be a speech act. When a performative is used, this otherwise implicit intention to represent is simply made explicit. That is why the appropriate performative can be added to a speech act without changing its content. Since there are five kinds of speech act, there are five basic intentions to represent, each of which can be made explicit by preceding the speech act with the appropriate performative: In uttering 'the car is washed,' I *assert* that the car is washed, or In uttering 'I'm ordering you to wash the car!' I *order* you to wash the car. Note that declaration is an interesting case in that every case involves a kind of a double-declaration: In saying 'I dub thee a knight' I declare that I declare (dub) you a knight. Thus, the possibility of declaration is founded on a kind of essential human capacity which underlies the very possibility of meaningful communication.

CHAPTER 7

ON THE MEANING OF MEANING: CRITICAL REMARKS

A NEW CONCEPTION OF MEANING

With the publication of *Intentionality* (1983) Searle reevaluates the basic account of meaning as found in *Speech Acts* (1969). In the earlier account, an action (such as the production of sound) is meaningful if it is done with the intention to communicate with the hearer. This communication involves the attempt to produce in the hearer, by some conventional means, knowledge of the speaker's intentional state (the sincerity condition).

In *Intentionality*, Searle reconsiders and revises the extension of the term "meaning" to accord with the semanticist. The most explicit treatment of the move is found in his article, "Meaning, Communication, and Representation" (1986), where Searle narrates the shift in his understanding of the meaning of meaning.

> Like most speech act theorists I have analysed meaning in terms of communication. The intentions that are the essence of meaning are intentions to produce effects on hearers, that is, they are intentions to communicate. But it now seems to me . . . that in at least one sense of "meaning," communication is derived from meaning rather than constitutive of meaning. Communication, one might say, is a consequence of meaning, but meaning exists independently of the intention to communicate that meaning. As a preliminary formulation, I shall argue that a speaker's uttering something and meaning something by it consists in the speaker's uttering something with the intention that his utterance should represent the world in one or more of the possible illocutionary

modes, and that the intention to communicate is the intention that these meaning intentions should be recognized by the hearer.[1]

According to his revised view, a sound, mark, or gesture is meaningful when it represents the world as being a certain way. Meaning is a function of the intention to represent. According to his old view, however, Searle sees meaning as a function of communication. If an audience happens to be present, and is privy to the speaker's intended meaning, then the speaker may further be said to communicate. With this move Searle decisively breaks the link between the concept of meaning and the concept of communication. Contra Grice, no longer is the illocutionary intention to communicate a necessary condition for a speaker's meaning something by an action.

There is a way of looking at this shift which minimizes its disruptive pull in reconciling Searle's earlier and later accounts of language.

> Notice . . . that this account of meaning and communication is in no way inconsistent with the view that the fundamental purpose of language is communication. Language provides us with public systems of representation, and thereby allows representations to be readily communicated from one speaker-hearer to another in virtue of their common knowledge of the rules of language.[2]

The later Searle is a semanticist about *meaning*. However, he appears to remain a communication-intention theorist insofar as *language* is involved. In order to use language, a speaker must intend to communicate with the hearer using a conventional system of rules. In spite of the awkwardness of disentangling the closely associated notions of meaning and language, almost the entirety of the Gricean analysis of speech acts remains intact, except for two qualifications: First, no longer can the three illocutionary intentions be considered conditions of speaker *meaning*. They rather specify the conditions under which an action counts as a speech act, and speech acts are associated with language use or communication. Second, while the fundamental purpose of language may be communication, this capacity is dependent on the more primitive capacity to mean something, which now has nothing to do with communication.

> The mistake was to suppose that the speaker's communication intentions and speaker meaning were identical. . . . On my present

account the primary meaning intentions are intentions to represent and they are independent of and prior to the intention to communicate those representations. A primary-meaning intention is an intention to represent; a communication intention is an intention that the hearer should know the representing intention.[3]

It is clear that in his later account, a sound, mark, or action counts as meaningful when it represents the world, a la the semanticist. Communication is secondary. As we saw in the last chapter, a sound, mark, or action comes to represent the world by way of a sincerity condition, the intention that the sincerity condition causes the utterance and an intention to represent.

How did Searle come to construe meaning in terms of representation rather than communication? He construes the shift as a natural extension of the criticism directed against Grice in *Speech Acts*, discussed above. Reviewing those objections in "Meaning, Communication, and Representation," Searle asks himself: "But now the question forces itself on us: if my objections to Grice are really valid why can't I extend them to my own account?"

Recall Searle's original criticism of Grice: if meaning involves the intention to communicate, what is the purpose of communication? Confining our attention to assertives, for Grice, saying something and meaning it requires that the speaker intends to *convince* the hearer that p is the case. Searle disagrees: to convince someone that p is the case requires first that they understand what "p" signifies and that the speaker believes that p is the case. Meaning something, thus, only requires that the speaker communicates their belief that p, which is possible without further intending that the hearer believe p. It may also be the case that the speaker intends that the hearer also believe that is the case, but that perlocutionary intention is not necessary to saying something and meaning it.

To both illustrate and support this claim, Searle has us consider the case of speaking out of duty, where the speaker says something without the intention to convince the hearer. Analogously, the author of a philosophy book presents reasons for believing an assertion. But the fact that the assertion was made does not imply an additional reason to believe it. This shows that there is a gap between a speaker's intention that an audience understands an assertion and the further perlocutionary intention that the audience believes it. To say something and mean it only requires the first, illocutionary intention.

In the decades that followed the publication of *Speech Acts,* Searle realized that this same strategy could be amplified to target his own early views:

> I argued against Grice that one can say some thing and mean it and still not intend to produce any response or action by the hearer. But why can there not be cases where one says something, means it, and does not intend to produce understanding in the hearer?[4]

In other words, if it is possible to mean something without intending certain perlocutionary effects, then it might be possible to mean something without intending to produce illocutionary effects—communication. On Searle's new view, meaning only requires the speaker's intention that some sound, mark, or action represent. Since that sound, mark, or action is the result of a further locutionary intention, Searle sometimes says that meaning involves the imposition of conditions of satisfaction on conditions of satisfaction—that is, the imposition of a capacity to represent on locutionary effects, e.g. mere sounds, marks, or gestures.

This is a remarkable admission. Without renouncing any of the structural features of the overall portrait of communication, the shift in emphasis is tantamount to a rejection of the communication-intention tradition. Of course we *can* communicate. But this is an ancillary function which anyway requires the ability to use mere words, marks, and actions to represent. In other words, following the semanticist, communication is to meaning or representation as pragmatics is to semantics: pragmatics is cast off as a secondary and derivative extension of semantics, the capacity to represent as being a certain way.

How can a shift in emphasis amount to a rejection of a tradition? Searle's move can be roughly schematized as shown in Figure 7.1.

The basic idea is that for Grice (thin line in Figure 7.1), someone can't be said to mean something by a sound unless the speaker intends to convince the hearer of a belief, and the hearer comes to understand what the speaker's belief is. If the hearer actually becomes convinced of the belief, then, a sound is not just meaningful, but successful. Searle, in *Speech Acts* (thick dashed line), only requires that in order for a sound to be meaningful, the speaker has the illocutionary intention that the hearer understands the expression (the sound which counts as representing p). For this it is *necessary* that the sound

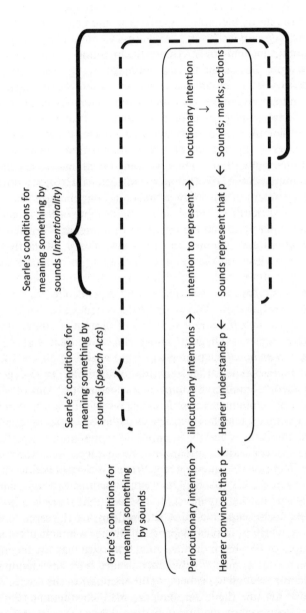

become an expression (by means of the intention to represent). But in order for the speech act to be *successful*, this expression must cause understanding or illocutionary effects in the hearer. Finally, in his later work, *Intentionality* and "Meaning, Communication, and Representation," meaning only requires the intention that a sound represent. In order for a sound to be meaningful it is not necessary for the speaker to further intend one effect or another on the hearer. An intention to represent is successful if sounds come to have conditions of satisfaction under some force or other. A speaker *may* intend to produce illocutionary or perlocutionary effects on the hearer, but this requires the application of a separate intention to communicate (illocutionary intentions). Thus, meaning intentions are screened off from communication (illocutionary) intentions. However, note that while the referent of the concept "meaning" has changed, the overall account or structure of speech acts remains more or less intact.

Searle's later view, that the intention to represent is possible without the intention to communicate but not visa versa, is exactly analogous to the view that the (locutionary) intention to make sounds, marks, or gestures is possible without the intention to represent but not vice versa. And this is correct when "dependency" flags a causal or ontological relation. This chain of dependency also helps explain why Searle shrinks the earlier accounts of meaning to the core intention to represent (see Diagram, above). However, there is also a *justificatory* or *functional* relation in which the chains of dependency are exactly inversed. The earlier intention to represent justifies or motivates someone's making a sound, mark, or gesture. And the earlier intention to communicate justifies someone's intention to represent. In other words, while the speaker had the intention to communicate because$_e$ the speaker had the intention to represent, it is equally true that the speaker had the intention to represent because$_j$ the speaker had the intention to communicate.[5] When Grice cites perlocutionary intentions as the key to meaning, it is the justificatory continuum of dependency that he has in mind. The fact that there is a sense in which the locutionary intention is dependent on the representation intention, which is, in turn, dependent on the communication intention may also be what motivates Austin to state that "in general the locutionary act as much as the illocutionary is an abstraction only: every genuine speech act is both. (This is similar to the way in which the phatic act, the rhetic act, &c., are mere abstractions.)"[6] To say that the locutionary intention or the illocutionary intention are *abstractions* is to point out that what can be screened off in thought does not always imply genuine autonomy.

IS SEARLE'S ORIGINAL CRITICISM OF GRICE COMPELLING?

I will argue that Searle's rearticulation of the concept of meaning, as found in *Intentionality*, may be a mistake even by Searle's own lights.

For Grice and the early Searle, meaning is specified in terms of communication, in terms of intended illocutionary or even perlocutionary effects. But where the early Searle thought the conditions of satisfaction are properly illocutionary, Grice contends that the speaker aims to produce a perlocutionary effect—namely, for assertives, to convince the speaker of the truth of the assertion.

However, the early Searle and Grice are not simply providing different answers to the same question; they are asking different questions. Grice asks, which effects are among an assertion's *typical* conditions of satisfaction? The early Searle asks, what are among an assertion's *minimal* conditions of satisfaction? Their answers are perlocutionary and illocutionary effects, respectively. I will argue that the early Searle has, even by his own terms, misled himself in focusing on an assertion's illocutionary effects as the defining mark of an assertion. This, in turn, prompts the later Searle to further truncate the notion of meaning in *Intentionality* and "Meaning, Communication, and Representation."

It is worth stepping back and surveying the metaphilosophical presuppositions against which Searle's early criticism of Grice gains traction. There are, in general, two approaches to analyzing a concept. We can look at *all* the instances which fall under a concept and try to specify the properties which they all have in common (their necessary conditions). Or we can look at the central, paradigm cases of a concept and specify the properties which *those* cases have in common. *All tables*, perhaps, have a horizontal surface. But a typical, *paradigmatic table* has a horizontal surface, plus four legs.[7]

Now consider these two approaches when the concept under consideration is that of *meaning*. What Searle has done is identify cases—speaking out of a sense of duty or philosophizing—in which a speaker is not trying to convince the audience of anything, but which nevertheless seems to involve meaningful assertion. Let's take for granted that the counterexamples are successful—that, for example, in speaking out of duty, the speaker does not in fact have the intention to convince the hearer of anything (rather than simply an expectation that this intention will go unsatisfied). Searle assumes that such counterexamples mandate a revision of the proposed criteria: the speaker, in order to speak meaningfully, need only intend to produce an illocutionary rather than perlocutionary effect. Searle is after a set of necessary and jointly sufficient conditions for what might minimally count as a meaningful assertion's possible conditions of satisfaction.

However, there are other ways to understand the significance of the counterexamples which would not mandate jettisoning Grice's account. Counterexamples can easily be dismissed as nonparadigmatic or borderline; the theorist might only point out the proposed criteria were never intended to comprehensively cover all conceivable instances of meaningful assertion. Indeed, saying something out of duty is uncontroversially a derivative case of assertion. The second case of philosophizing just misses the point; the perlocutionary effect that Grice considered indicative of an assertion's conditions of satisfaction, is simply that the speaker be convinced of the truth of what is said; it is incidental whether the speaker further intends that the hearer be convinced simply by virtue of the fact that it was said. The fact that reasons are required to convince the hearer of p's truth does not mean the speaker did not assert p with the intention that the hearer believe p.

Furthermore, the philosophical case may itself be unparadigmatic. Typically, the fact that someone said something is a reason to accept it as true. Sometimes, as when we philosophize, the speaker aims to bring about a perlocutionary effect by way of a battery of explicit reasons. Indeed, focusing on reason-giving enterprises, such as science and philosophy, can obscure the fact that, in the vast majority of assertions that we encounter in our day-to-day lives, the fact that someone says something itself constitutes a reason to believe it. When a friend tells me they are not feeling well, that is, ceteris paribus, a reason to believe that they are not feeling well.[8]

Indeed, Searle himself makes several claims that would appear to endorse the view that the fact that a speaker says something amounts to a prima facie reason to believe it. If a newsanchor tells of a bombing in Baghdad, that is typically reason to believe it. I believe a computer technician who tells me that my operating system is burdened with a malicious computer virus. If my bill says that I owe the gas company some amount of money, that is typically a reason to believe it.

In *Rationality in Action* Searle states that a speaker's assertion implies a commitment to the truth of that assertion. But if the speaker is necessarily committed to the truth of the assertion that, for example, it's raining, then this constitutes a reason for the hearer to believe it is raining (and not just that the speaker believes that it is raining). Justification is, perhaps, a norm of assertion. Tellingly, Searle describes this commitment to truth as a condition for *meaning* something:

> [I]f he is not just uttering the sentence but actually saying that it is raining, if he actually, means that it is raining, then he must intend that the utterance satisfy truth conditions, the conditions of satisfaction with a downward direction of fit that it is raining. . . . And he is not neutral vis-a-vis truth or falsity, because his claim is a claim to truth.[9]

By Searle's own admission, meaning something implies that the speaker believes it, and so constitutes a reason for the hearer's believing it. This relationship between truth and assertion has a converse aspect. A hearer is not entitled to doubt an assertion unless there is a reason to doubt it. Skepticism needs to be motivated by what Grice calls a "doubt-or-denial condition."[10] There must be, according to Austin, "a special reason to doubt the testimony" or assertion of another: "we are entitled to trust others, except in so far as there is some concrete reason to distrust them."[11] The default position is belief, unless there is a special, additional reason to doubt it.

The significance of the purported counterexamples depends on whether or not the philosopher is aiming to specify the boundary conditions of a concept or the paradigm case. Since Searle is worried that saying something out of duty or philosophical assertion is not covered by Grice's conditions, it appears that Searle is after the minimal, necessary, and sufficient conditions of a speech act. However, this move is surprising, as it is discontinuous with his typical approach to philosophizing. For example, in discussing the concept of reference, Searle dismisses the force of certain counterexamples to his own view according to the following rationale:

> These [counterexamples] seem to lack many of the features which give point to paradigm definite references. A common mistake in philosophy is to suppose there must be a right and unequivocal answer to such questions, or worse yet, to suppose that unless there is a right and unequivocal answer, the concept of referring is

a worthless concept. The proper approach, I suggest, is to examine those cases which constitute the center of variation of the concept of referring and then examine the borderline cases in light of their similarities and differences from the paradigms. As long as we are aware of both similarities and differences, it may not matter much whether we call such cases referring or not.[12]

If concepts are assumed to be well defined, then counterexamples can invalidate a proposed theory. However, if Searle is aiming for the paradigmatic, the "center of variation of the concept," counter-examples may be dismissed as marginal or borderline cases which the account was never intended to cover in the first place. Looking at the concept of *meaning*, even if we assume that speaking out of duty or philosophizing are counterexamples, Searle himself is typically reluctant to see concepts as sharply defined; he rather attempts to provide analysis of central cases, granting, as in the case of the concept of reference, that there will be borderline instances. It is unclear why, in the case of the concept of meaning, Searle changes methodological strategies.

Searle explicitly flags the fact that his method in *Speech Acts* is at odds with his typical approach to philosophizing: "I have used different methods for different tasks. When I did the theory of speech acts, I tried to analyze the necessary and sufficient conditions for the performance of a speech act and the utterance of a sentence."[13] Given this, Searle is able to criticize Grice by way of a method of counter-examples. But what makes the topic of speech acts, as opposed to reference, particularly suitable to this mode of philosophizing?

The debate between Grice and the early Searle is only superficially a debate about which among a meaningful assertion's many effects constitute its proper conditions of satisfaction (illocutionary or per-locutionary). The debate rather hinges, not on the facts, but on the adopted model of philosophical inquiry. These are metaphilosophical differences disguised as a factual dispute; this is a methodological debate in drag.

IS SEARLE'S CRITICISM OF SEARLE COMPELLING?

Searle's *Intentionality* and "Meaning, Communication, and Representation" explicitly reframes the core features of his philosophy of language, rejecting the principles of the communication-intention tradition, within which Searle had taken himself to be working. In this section I will argue that Searle's semantic turn was just, in fact, a working out of a certain trajectory already begun in *Speech Acts*. As such, the viability of the semanticist turn is strongly dependent on the viability of his original criticisms of Grice.

Earlier, in *Speech Acts*, Searle argued that in order for an assertion to be meaningful, the speaker need only intend to provoke illocutionary, rather than perlocutionary, effects in the hearer. Later, in *Intentionality*, Searle wondered whether it was necessary to intend to produce any effect in the hearer whatsoever. Following the semanticist, a gesture, sound, or mark is meaningful if the speaker imposes the capacity to represent the world, via conditions of satisfaction, on those brute facts. Since the speaker also made the sound, mark, or gesture, Searle describes the meaning intention or intention to represent in terms of the imposition of conditions of satisfaction on conditions of satisfaction.

Because Searle iterates the critical strategy directed against Grice, this second move can only be as successful as the original move against Grice. But, I argued that Grice was not after *minimal* conditions for an utterance's meaning something; rather, his account of meaning aimed at saying something about the nature of central, paradigm cases of meaning. What is so uncanny about Searle's appeal to counterexamples, in the service of generating a set of necessary and jointly sufficient conditions for meaning, is that the approach seems so un-Searlean.

Speaking out of duty is an unparadigmatic case of assertion and so of limited use when the aim is to articulate the conditions by which assertions are typically meaningful. What are the cases which motivate Searle's later account of meaning, in terms of the intention to represent rather than the intention to communicate or convince? In the article, Searle imagines a case wherein an English speaker communicates to a hearer who does not speak English, the fact that the speaker's crankshaft is broken. The speaker does this by way of a drawing. To *mean* something, according to his later view, it is only necessary that the speaker intends the marks to represent the fact that the crankshaft is broken.

Furthermore, in the example, the representation of the broken crankshaft is clearly separable from the communication of the fact that the crankshaft is broken. This is brought out by the fact that one can represent without communicating, or without any intention to communicate. For example, I might just draw the picture to have a picture of my broken crankshaft without any desire or intention to communicate the fact that the crankshaft is broken to anyone. Nor does it seem correct to say in such cases that I am communicating with my future self, or acting as if I were communicating with someone else. For I might, for example, deliberately draw the picture with the intention that there be no communication at all. I might intend to destroy the picture or draw it in disappearing ink, for example.

In *Speech Acts*, Searle used the case of speaking out of duty to show that we can communicate without the intention to convince, so showing that meaning is not necessarily a matter of perlocutionary intentions. Analogously, in his later texts, Searle uses the case of soliloquy to show that we can mean something without intending to communicate.

But, in response, if speaking out of duty is an unparadigmatic case of meaningful assertion, then soliloquy or the production of private language are surely likewise exceptional cases of meaningful assertion. The conclusion is somewhat akin to the ecologist who says that crows are not black because several albino crows have been observed. This would be true *if* the aim is to provide necessary and jointly sufficient conditions of all cases of meaning something. But this is hardly paradigmatic of Searle's approach to philosophizing. Should one build an account of meaning on the basis of outliers?

CHAPTER 8

THE CONSTRUCTION OF SOCIAL REALITY

ACTS THAT ACHIEVE THEIR AIMS BY CONVENTIONAL MEANS

Words do things; we utter noises with the intention of achieving certain purposes or functions.[1] Orders and commands attempt to get the hearer to do something. In asserting something, a speaker communicates by representing a state of affairs and may further do so with the intention of communicating with the hearer.

Many of these functional effects are such that I can bring about their realization through nonlinguistic means. I could request that someone move out of my way or else I could push them out of the way. I could tell someone that I purchased a jacket or I could simply show them the new jacket.

What distinguishes my pushing someone out the way from a request or order that they move out of my way, given that both actions are undertaken with the same purpose in mind? Either action may fail to achieve its intended purpose. The speech act may be less rude but it need not be. An important difference is that the speech act works by means of a *conventional* aspect, as required by Searle's third illocutionary intention. If I succeed in pushing someone out of the way, my success is entirely a function of the vector sum of the various forces acting on the person pushed. A resistance on the part of the person pushed or even a strong crosswind might undermine my attempts. However if I request that a person move, my success is determined, in part, by whether or not the hearer *understands* what I said—understands that the noises "please move" *count as* a request to move (in English). This illocutionary effect is a means by which the ultimate perlocutionary effect—that the person does not just understand the request but actually moves—is achieved.

As seen in the last chapter, we typically do not talk *simply* with the intention of producing understanding of what I meant—the illocutionary effect. The principle, intended effect or point of my saying something is perlocutionary. In asking someone to move I do not just want them to know that I have asked them to move—I want them to move. In telling someone I bought a new jacket, I don't want them simply to believe that I believe I bought a new jacket. I rather say this with the expectation that they will believe that it is the case.

If the intended function of a speech act has a conventional aspect, this draws attention to the fact that there is nothing nomologically necessary about the means by which the effect was achieved. As an English speaker I might ask someone to move by saying "please move" but it *could* have been another series of sounds: a German says, "Bitte, berühren Sie sich." The conventionality of a speech act gets at the fact that there is an aspect of the speech act that could have been otherwise, that the sounds, "please move," are in a sense, arbitrary. However, if I push someone, they *must* move given that I have shoved them with enough force; the means by which the intended outcome is achieved is not dependent on the conventions within which the actors are working but it has the force of physical necessity.[2]

The conventions which allow me to pursue various aims and effects take the form of what Searle calls "constitutive rules." Generally, in the English language, the sounds "please move" count as a request that the hearer move. This is the constitutive rule about how the sounds "please move" are used. In another language the same sounds are meaningless or could, at least in principle, mean something else altogether.

All constitutive rules have the form "X counts as Y in context C," where X is a brute fact and Y is an institutional fact. C is a contextual marker. Constitutive rules are conventional in the sense that there is nothing necessary about the fact that X is linked with Y; in a different community or context the same institutional fact might be linked with an entirely different set of brute facts so that English speakers and German speakers use different sounds in order to achieve the same effect.

Part of what the "X counts as Y in C" formula is meant to convey is that institutional facts (Y) are built on or in some way dependent on a set of brute facts (X). Institutional reality, including language, is not free-floating, but is rather founded on a base of physical stuff, including particles in fields of force. Thus part of the project of *The Construction of Social Reality* is to show how our social and institutional reality can be founded on the physical base. "Since our investigation is ontological, i.e., about how social facts exist, we need to figure out how social reality fits into our overall ontology, i.e., how the existence of social facts relates to other things that exist."[3]

This returns us to the familiar ontological quandary that frames most of Searle's philosophical enterprises: how can a certain puzzling fact be reconciled with a less-puzzling fundamental ontology? How can the manifest image be reconciled with the scientific image? In this case the puzzling facts are institutional facts—language, money, the office of the president.

In Chapter 6 we saw Searle's answer to this question, when the explanandum was language. Sounds count as representations if a speaker imposes conditions of satisfaction on those sounds. When this happens the sounds themselves come to have a derived intentionality—the ability to represent the world under a certain force. In other words, Searle answers the ontological puzzle of language by appealing to the remarkable intentional ability to impose conditions of satisfaction (represent the world as being a certain way) on conditions of satisfaction (the sounds).

But language is just one kind of institutional fact. How is money or the presidency possible in a world which consists of particles in fields of force and minds? In *The Construction of Social Reality*, Searle generalizes his answer as it applies to language so as to cover the entire institutional sphere. But where a language user imposes conditions of satisfaction on a sound, mark, or gesture, Searle will argue that for institutional facts in general, the agent likewise imposes functions (Y) on some brute fact or other (X). This is the basic insight captured by the *X counts as Y in C* formula.

INSTITUTIONAL FACTS

What are institutional facts (Y) and how are they distinguished from the brute facts (X) on which they are instantiated?

Three Kinds of Institutional Facts

We will be in a position to see what an institutional fact is when we get a sense of the kind of institutional facts there are. Institutional facts can be imposed on three categories of brute facts: actions, persons, and other kinds of objects or events.

As we have seen, speech acts are institutional facts. Other actions, which are not overtly linguistic, are also institutional facts. For example a person could be dubbed a knight by a queen; the movement of the sword is probably not a speech act but is an institutional fact. The act of punching a hole in a certain card in a voting booth is, likewise, a nonlinguistic institutional fact. In these examples institutional facts are actions, although not all actions are institutional facts. Simply punching a hole in a card or pushing someone out of the way are noninstitutional brute facts. Punching a hole in a certain card in a certain context or else saying, "Please get out of my way," are institutional facts. A task is to distinguish merely punching a hole in a card from voting.

Sometimes the brute fact on which an institutional fact is instantiated is a person. When people are construed as biological organisms, they are seen simply as brute objects. But these organisms are also citizens, professors, students, presidents, queens, knights, members of the armed services, and so on. As such, these biological organisms (X) are construed in terms of institutional facts (Y). In a kind of Hobbesian state of nature, there are no citizens or presidents or soldiers—we are reduced to conscious, biological beasts. Searle's aim is to give us the means by which to distinguish the queen from a woman wearing robes and a metal circlet on her head. He does this by explaining how queenhood, or any other institutional fact, is possible.

Finally, objects and events, besides actions and persons, can be institutional facts. A green piece of paper with certain markings (X) can count as money (Y) in certain circumstances. In other circumstances, shells and feathers or certain kinds of rocks might count as money. A certain noise counts as an air-raid warning. A gold circlet counts as a crown. When utterances are causally separated from the movement of the larynx which produced them, as in a recording, it may be more convenient to treat them as an event rather than part of the action, so that if I hear "call home" on my voicemail, it is preferable to say that those noises-*qua*-event (X) count as a request or order (Y). So far as the task of getting clear on what institutional facts are, nothing much banks on a precise distinction between the various brute substrata of actions, persons, and others sorts of objects or events.

So actions, people, and other kinds of objects and events can be the bearers of institutional facts. What becomes clear in these examples is that the institutional fact has a kind of significance that goes beyond the brute fact on which it is founded. Money is something more than the stuff it is made of. "Stop!" isn't just movement of vocal chords and the noise they produce. A queen is more than just a woman. It is also clear that whatever money is, in addition to being a green piece of paper and ink, it is not another *thing* that is somehow added to the paper. But neither is money simply reducible to the brute stuff out of which it is made, as the institutional materialist might have it.

So what *is* institutional reality?

In introducing the idea of an institutional fact in *The Construction of Social Reality*, Searle tends to focus on things like money, which are founded on nonpersonal objects and events. Money is an excellent example insofar as it successfully leverages our intuition that money is not just a particular amalgam of paper and ink; we can also see how money might be constituted by a variety of different brute facts. But the money example is also misleading. Searle recognizes this when he writes, "Social objects are always . . . constituted by social acts; and, in a sense, *the object is just the continuous possibility of the activity*. A twenty dollar bill, for example, is a standing possibility of paying for something."[4] Then, much later in the text, he changes the emphasis again when he writes that "the category of people, including groups, is fundamental in the sense that the imposition of status-functions on objects and events works only in relation to people. . . . It is not the five dollar bill as an object that matters, but rather that the possessor of the five dollar bill now has a certain power that he or she did not otherwise have."[5] Rather than follow Searle's pedagogical model, which begins with objects and events, we will begin with the category of people and their actions as our primary institutional exemplars.

Institutional Facts as Functional Phenomena

Having provided a list of examples, can we formulate criteria by which we are able to distinguish institutional facts from noninstitutional facts?

Looking at the physical structure of the institutional fact will not help: as mentioned, ontologically speaking, an institutional fact is nothing more than the brute fact it is instantiated on. The queen is in some sense just a woman, a biological organism.

We might then try to distinguish institutional facts from noninstitutional facts according to what they *do*—what kind of effects they bring about. Both brute and institutional facts stand in causal relations with other facts in the world. Moreover, since both brute and institutional facts may have the same consequences, it seems that we can't look to the kind of effect brought about as a means to distinguish the two kinds of fact. For example both an executioner and a falling piano might cause a death, but only the former is an institutional fact.

There is, nevertheless, an important difference in the death that resulted from the hand of an executioner and the death that resulted from the fall of a piano. The killing is a functional effect of the executioner but not so for the piano. The executioner exists for the purpose of killing people, which is not the case for the piano. *Institutional facts are functional entities*; they exist for the *purpose* of bringing about some effect or other: money facilitates exchange, an assertion allows me to communicate a state of affairs, queens lead, executioners kill, and so on.

This functional nature gives part of the means by which to distinguish institutional facts from brute facts, such as rocks and rainbows, which have no function. The latter are not institutional facts.

However this criterion is of limited use, as there are many brute facts, such as hearts and livers, which have functions but are not institutional. Searle argues that we further exclude these so-called "nonagentive functions" from the sphere of the institutional on the grounds that such attributions make no reference to the specific purposes or interests of human beings. A heart may pump blood but its doing so can't be traced back to a network of values and purposes which are specifically our own; these effects exist quite independently of us. This stands in contrast to knives, chairs, money, queens, executioners, language, and so on, which would not exist *but for* the aims and desires of human beings. These "agentive functions" are created by human beings for their own purposes, and all institutional facts are agentive functions.

But the remaining agentive functions are still not necessarily institutional. Searle claims that walls, which have the function of prohibiting trespass, are not institutional facts. I can turn on the stove in order to cook, but my doing so is not an institutional fact. Indeed,

Searle even wishes to exclude certain forms of social or cooperative action—as when animals coordinate in a hunt—from the sphere of the institutional. So, some agentive functions are social facts and some of those are institutional facts. In the next section we will discuss the criteria by which agentive functions count as social facts and the narrower criterion by which some of those social facts count as institutional facts.

This taxonomy of phenomena can be diagrammed as shown in Figure 8.1:

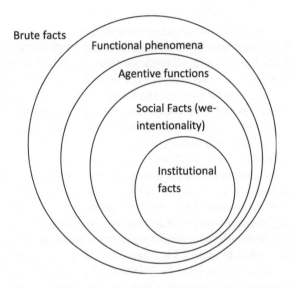

Note that according to the chart, institutional facts are a kind of brute fact—which constitutes Searle's fundamental ontology—just as cars are a kind of vehicle. This is in some sense right, as Searle's ultimate aim is to locate social and institutional facts within an ontology of brute facts. Searle thinks that "social facts in general, and institutional facts especially, are hierarchically structured. Institutional facts exist, so to speak, on top of brute physical facts."[6] Nevertheless, throughout much of the text he talks of social and institutional facts in *contrast to* brute facts. If a car is a kind of vehicle, it would be nonsensical to then contrast cars with vehicles. However, when Searle makes this contrast, he merely means to say that social and institutional facts may be contrasted with other brute facts which do not have this status. This is akin to comparing cars with vehicles which are not cars, which is unproblematic even if we agree that cars are kinds of vehicles.

Institutional Facts and Deontic Powers: The Status Function

Granting that institutional facts are agentive functions, how does Searle distinguish those agentive functions which are institutional facts (money, voting, queens) from those agentive functions that are not (knives, chairs, walls)?

Before answering this question we need to make a preliminary distinction between two kinds of intentionality.

Searle distinguishes two kinds of intentions with which action is undertaken. My attempt to cook involves a kind of singular, "I" intentionality. Social and institutional facts, by contrast, implicate a collective, "we" intentionality. As a member of a football team, *we* intend to win, make it to the finals, and so on. This we-intention exists within the head of each player on the team; in granting the possibility of we-intentionality we ought not imagine it as a kind of singular superthought or borg-consciousness, hovering over the heads of the participants. In drawing our attention to the possibility of we-intentionality, Searle only wishes to remind us of the kind of thoughts which accompany collective action, whether in playing sports, singing in a church choir, contributing to an online encyclopedia, completing the agenda in a department meeting, and so on. In these cases, what is required is a set of collective purposes around which we organize, at least to some extent, our own actions and decisions.

To return to the football example, in aiming to accomplish the team's collective purpose of scoring a touchdown or winning the game, each player also exercises singular I-intentions. While I and the rest of the team each we-intend to score a touchdown, I, as a receiver, may I-intend to catch the ball where the quarterback may I-intend to throw the ball. But these I-intentions are an extension of, and can only be understood against, a shared we-intention. In this way, while both, in playing football, blocking and in cooking, turning on the stove are agentive, functional phenomena, only playing football is a *social fact* because only it operates within the scope of an overriding we-intention. Searle stipulates that any activity done by way of a we-intention is what qualifies some agentive functions as social facts. As we will see, however, not all social facts are, further, institutional facts. Obviously, turning on the stove could be a social fact if, for example, I did so in my capacity as a member of a team of chefs. But then I turn on the stove in order that *we* might prepare the requested menu items (the we-intention's condition of satisfaction).

My turning on the stove is an agentive, functional phenomenon: I do so with the aim of cooking something (the condition of satisfaction). But if I am cooking for myself this is not an institutional fact because it is not a social fact—the action is not guided by the required we-intentionality. What about the actions of animals in a pack, who coordinate various actions in order to hunt prey? These actions are functional. They are, moreover, social actions because they appear to be guided by a we-intention. But these actions are not institutional facts.

So if social facts involve collective intentionality, how might we distinguish institutional facts from mere social facts?

Early in *The Construction of Social Reality* Searle gives an answer to this question which is telling but ultimately inadequate. Searle has us imagine a wall that has been built by a tribe to keep out intruders. This wall is a social fact, as it has been built, stone by stone, with the collective intention of protecting the tribe. But the wall is not an institutional fact. Now imagine that, over time, the wall deteriorates until there is nothing but a circle of stones around the village. This circle of stone is, for Searle, an institutional fact. Given that the wall and line of stones serve the same collective, agentive function, what distinguishes them? Searle marks the difference between mere social facts and institutional facts by suggesting that the latter can perform its function in a way that is not dependent on the physical structure of the artifact in question. The wall does not just keep people out; it acquires what Searle calls a "status function" when it performs that function in a way that is quite independent of its physical constitution.

We can mark the difference between the two kinds of functions by looking at the terms we would use to characterize functional breakdown. If a wall, as social fact, only performs its function by virtue of its physical structure alone, and it failed to perform that function (it was not high enough, it was weak) so that members of a rival tribe were able to cross it, we would describe the wall as *dysfunctional*.

However, if members of a rival tribe cross a circle of stones, the problem is not with the stones. They see stones, they know that they mark a boundary, and they cross it anyway. The stones are not dysfunctional; rather the members of this tribe are *remiss*. We will address the difference between these kinds of breakdown in greater detail below.

Notice that money nicely exemplifies the requirement that institutional facts serve their function in a way which is not dependent on their physical structure alone: while a green piece of paper with certain markings facilitates exchange, its physical structure is only incidentally related to that function. Speech acts also fit this requirement: if the officer says, "Show me your passport," and that order succeeds by prompting the traveler to show the passport, the officer's perlocutionary intention is not satisfied simply by virtue of the physical structure of the sounds. Money, speech acts, and the ring of stones thus perform a function in an importantly different way than does a wall or a chair, even when a we-intention is present. Indeed, this requirement is a generalization of the conventionality requirement, (the third illocutionary intention) so far as language is concerned: the ring of stones conventionally means, *keep out*.

I have elsewhere argued that the requirement that institutional facts perform their function in a way that is independent of their physical structure cannot work.[7] Granting that the circle of stones is an institutional fact, imagine that the tribe rebuilds the wall. Does the border then *revert* to a mere social fact? No. Putting the same point more concretely, the United States is currently building a fence that extends across its border with Mexico. This border is uncontroversially an institutional fact. But, contra Searle, this *status* is not contingent on whether or not there happens to be a physical barrier between the countries. An economic refugee may climb the fence. The fence may be *dysfunctional*, but it also is the case that the refugee remains, in some sense, *remiss*. Searle is mistaken to think that he can make a reliable distinction between institutional facts and other kinds of functional facts, including social ones, by appeal to the physical structure of those facts alone.

There is another problem with Searle's physicalist criterion. The reader may have noticed that the kinds of facts that most easily accommodate this criteria are not people nor actions, but other kinds of objects—stones, sounds, and certain pieces of paper. But these objects are not paradigm cases of institutional facts; they are, as

Searle notes, placeholders of patterns of activity. An execution—an action—is an institutional fact and so distinguished from a mere killing. But note that the arm movement which drives the blade, in the case of a beheading, performs the execution in virtue of the physical structure alone. While not all institutional actions are like this, as when the queen dubs a man a knight, it is clear that Searle cannot distinguish institutional facts from other kinds of functions simply by appeal to the physical properties of the event in question.

This misleading picture arises because Searle places undue emphasis on institutional *objects*, such as money and a line of stones, as paradigm cases of institutional facts. One problem with this is that objects cannot be *remiss*; under certain conditions, a nonexecutioner would be remiss in killing someone whereas an executioner would be remiss in not killing someone. Walls and knives are dysfunctional but executioners and queens can be remiss. When we move the emphasis to persons and their actions, the possibility of various kinds of functional breakdown constitutes a more suitable principle of differentiation, which aims to distinguish institutional from social facts. Searle seems more cognizant of this in the latter half of *The Construction of Social Reality*, which places much less emphasis on objects.

Institutional facts cannot be distinguished from social phenomena by appeal to the criterion that the institutional facts can perform their function independently of the physical structure of that fact. That institutional facts carry with them the possibility of remission, however, provides a clue as to the actual point of difference between institutional and social facts.

Consider the following two cases. First, a member of a pack of hyenas gets distracted in such a way that the group fails to catch the prey. Second, in the middle of an offensive drive, a receiver gets frustrated and walks off the football field thereby undermining the play. Both are social facts, but only the latter is institutional, and while the actions of both the hyena and the receiver are dysfunctional, only the latter is remiss. Why? Simply put, because only the receiver is capable of bearing what Searle calls "deontic power." Searle writes that

> [a]nimals running in a pack can have all the consciousness and collective intentionality they need. They can even have hierarchies and a dominant male; they can cooperate in the hunt, share their food, and even have pair bonding. But they cannot have marriages, property, or money. Why not? Because all these create institutional

forms of powers, rights, obligations, duties etc., and it is characteristic of such phenomena that they create reasons for action that
are independent of what you or I or anyone else is otherwise
inclined to do.[8]

Searle characterizes the deontic phenomena which underlie institutional facts, and distinguish them from social facts, as a kind of
power. Moreover, this power implies desire-independent reasons for
action. A queen who has the right to execute her subjects might be
said to be empowered to do so. Deontic power is likewise what com-
pels or obligates me to pay my taxes. The physical laws of the universe make certain actions possible or impossible. The deontic powers
indicative of institutional reality further constrain those nomological
possibilities by way of a complex system of rights and obligations.
People who, by their actions, violate the obligations that are ascribed
to them as a teacher, citizen, president, queen, executioner, receiver,
may be said to be remiss. As we will see, to be remiss is not simply to
fail to bring about a certain goal or function.

The deontic powers—rights and obligations—that underlie
institutional facts concern the *means* by which a person with an
institutional status brings about a function. By virtue of being a
teacher someone may exercise certain rights (assigning homework)
and meet certain obligations (assign a final grade); these rights and
obligations tend to be assigned with an eye toward the function of
teaching: the transmission of skills and knowledge via instruction.

Because a status function has both an end and a means, there are
at least two ways in which a person could *fail* to be a teacher. First,
they could fail to bring about the end or goal of teaching—instruction. Second, they could teach in the wrong way so that the means
by which instruction is brought about falls outside the scope of a
teacher's rights and obligations. These are to a large extent separable
from one another. U.S. Ambassador Jean Kirkpatrick said of John
Bolton, the controversial diplomat and former U.S. representative to
the United Nations: "He loves to tussle. He may do diplomatic jobs
for the U.S. government, but John is not a diplomat."[9] Kirkpatrick's
assessment of Bolton does *not* concern his *effectiveness* in resolving
transnational disputes; indeed, his ability to achieve certain results
is one of the reasons he keeps getting "diplomatic jobs." Bolton's
problem, rather, concerns the *means* by which he accomplishes these
ends. Bolton's hawkish tenacity is not sensitive enough to the deontic

powers constitutive of a status function of diplomat. Robert E. White, a former U.S. ambassador to El Salvador, elucidates some of these obligations in his criticism of Bolton: "Even the most forthright of [diplomats] have to have a certain reserve, a certain respect, courtesy, and understanding that you're dealing with politics and not theology. The whole point of diplomacy is to gain your ends without giving offense."[10] If Bolton is a bad diplomat, it is not because he is ineffective or dysfunctional (although he may be this), but it is because he is remiss—and remission concerns a failure to bring about a function within the scope of preassigned deontic powers.

The goodness of other, noninstitutional functional phenomena is evaluated in a way that is indifferent to the means. Where the means by which a certain function is brought about is *constitutive* of a status function, for a nonstatus function this means or mechanism is an accidental feature of the fact that some goal or purpose tends to be brought about. A heart is a heart simply by virtue of the fact that it pumps blood; that it happens to be made of muscle or plastic is an accidental, nonessential feature. Not so for institutional functions. To be a diplomat, it is not enough that one negotiates on behalf of a country; one has to do so in the right way—within a framework of assigned rights and obligations. To be a teacher, it is not enough that one instructs; one has to do so in the right way—disowning methods reliant on, for example, physical torture which, though possibly effective in instructing students, would render the teacher remiss. Such a teacher would be a bad (unvirtuous) teacher, even if they manage to induce learning.

Note that these powers are what distinguish Searle's view from that of the structural functionalist. While both Searle and the functionalist agree that social phenomena must be understood in terms of a network of purposes and functions, Searle further maintains that a subclass of these phenomena have an irreducible normative or deontic element, which cannot be paraphrased in terms of a distribution of functions. For the structural functionalist, remission is always construed in terms of mere dysfunction.

THE CREATION OF INSTITUTIONAL FACTS

Institutional facts are distinguished from brute facts in that the former imply a set of deontic powers exercised by some agent or other. But how do institutional facts come into existence?

We might begin by reviewing the distinction between ontologically objective and ontologically subjective phenomena, introduced in Chapter 2. Ontologically subjective entities, such as mental states,[11] depend on subjects for their existence, whereas ontologically objective entities, such as electrons and mountains, do not. Ontologically objective entities plus mental states constitute the entirety of the physical world, according to Searle's expanded notion of the physical. They are both part of Searle's fundamental ontology and are correctly regarded as brute facts, defined as those facts which "require no human institutions for their existence."[12]

The notion of the ontologically subjective, however, extends past the scope of the brute. If the ontologically subjective includes any fact which is dependent on a subject or agent, it will include the brute facts of our mental, qualitative states. But it will also include a number of other agent- or observer-dependent phenomena, including functional facts, social facts, and institutional facts.

How are institutional facts possible given an ontologically objective world of electrons in fields of force? Searle's quick answer: "We will use the 'mental,' so construed, to show how 'culture' is constructed out of 'nature.'"[13] In short, Searle bridges the gap between the ontologically objective world as described by science and the ontologically subjective, agent-dependent cultural world by way of another, more primitive ontologically subjective fact—the agent's mental states. Money and the presidency are possible because we make them possible; we, as conscious agents capable of sustaining intentional states, *impose* a status function on otherwise brute, blind, ontologically objective phenomena.

Searle's move, here, generalizes the intention to represent, discussed in Chapter 6. Recall that the intention to represent takes the conditions of satisfaction of a speaker's intentional state (sincerity condition) and imposes it on a brute sound, mark, or gesture.

The idea, in the case of institutional facts, is that not only do we have the ability to impose the capacity to represent on a brute phenomenon, but we also have the ability to impose a function and its attendant deontic powers on a brute phenomenon (most typically, another agent).

Searle's ontological categories can be represented as shown in Figure 8.2.

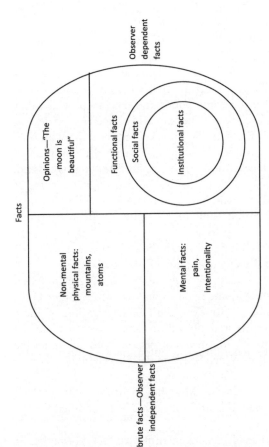

Facts

brute facts—Observer independent facts

Non-mental physical facts: mountains, atoms

Mental facts: pain, intentionality

Opinions—"The moon is beautiful"

Functional facts

Social facts

Institutional facts

Observer dependent facts

Observer dependent facts require intentionality. Mental facts are observer independent in the sense that pain does not require consciousness in order to exist; it is rather a way in which we can be conscious.

Only the category of non-mental physical facts are ontologically objective. The remaining facts, including mental facts, are ontologically subjective.

Only the category of opinions are epistemically subjective. The remaining facts, including all functional facts, are epistemically objective. The distinction between the epistemically subjective and the epistemically objective is less an ontological distinction than a distinction about the kinds of judgments we can have about facts.

ON THE CODIFIABILITY OF DEONTIC POWERS: A CRITICISM

If the assignment of rights and obligations are constitutive of institutional facts, how can things like money and a line of stones designating a political boundary be institutional facts? Pieces of paper and stones are not the sort of things to which we can ascribe deontic powers. Recall that institutional *objects* are not, for Searle, paradigm cases of institutionality. Searle writes that "it is not the five dollar bill as an *object* that matters, but rather that the *possessor* of the five dollar bill now has a certain power that he or she did not otherwise have."[14] Five dollar bills do not *have* rights and obligations; they rather aid in the distribution of certain rights and obligations, so that the possessor is entitled to certain goods and services to which they would not otherwise have access. They are also obliged not to destroy the currency. Similarly, the boundary markers either impose an obligation on noncitizens to not cross that marker or else flag the fact that the noncitizen will be without certain rights if that line is crossed. Again, institutional *objects* are derivative, nonparadigmatic cases of institutional facts and, as such, have potentially misleading features. In any case, it is clear that something's status as an institutional artifact has little or nothing to do with its categorical, structural, brute features, and everything to do with the collective imposition of deontic powers, either directly or indirectly, on a person.

There is, no doubt, something right about the suggestion that deontic powers help individuate institutional facts from other kinds of functional phenomena. However, the characterization of these powers in terms of rights and obligations may overarticulate the nature of the normative commitments of persons who fall under the scope of a status function. When Searle makes this claim he seems to have in mind highly codified institutions, such as marriage, the Presidency or a Japanese tea ceremony. Modeling institutionality on these cases, Searle requires that all institutions *could* be so codified.[15]

A test for the presence of genuine institutional facts is whether or not we could codify the rules explicitly. In the case of many institutional facts, such as property, marriage, and money, these indeed have been codified into explicit laws. Others, such as friendship, dates, and cocktail parties, are not so codified, but they could be. . . . Such institutional patterns could be codified if it mattered tremendously whether or not something was really a cocktail party or only a tea party. If the rights and duties of friendship suddenly became a matter of some grave legal or moral question, then we might imagine these informal institutions becoming codified explicitly, though of course explicit codification has its price. It deprives us of the flexibility, spontaneity, and informality that the practice has in its uncodified form.[16]

Notice that the first and last sentences of this passage nearly contradict one another. If codification has "its price," so that the codified institution does not exactly resemble the uncodified institution, what can we make of the requirement that all institutions *could* be codified into explicit rights and obligations? And if every institutional fact could be codified, why would doing so change or formalize the institution in question? Can the normative component of friendships, dates, and cocktail parties be formalized into explicit laws without remainder, as per Searle's requirement? Are cocktail parties just more *complicated* than a Japanese tea ceremony? By Searle's own account, the answer appears to be "no." Searle seems to correctly observe that institutional phenomena implicate deontic powers, which help govern the means by which certain functions are realized; but he appears to overarticulate and legalize the nature of that normative requirement when he maintains that we be able, at least in principle, to describe that normative component in terms of "explicit laws."

Dating or negotiating a cocktail party correctly is not simply a matter of adhering to, subconsciously or otherwise, myriad *rules*. I propose that it requires, rather, a kind of Aristotelian *social competence*. Thus, while institutional phenomena have a normative component, the characterization of those norms in terms of codifiable rights and obligations misses the extreme context-dependency of those norms. A host who serves milk at a cocktail party is not quite remiss but rather exhibits an error in judgment. Such a host is not in violation of an obligation, so much as what Alasdair MacIntyre calls "defective in doing or being good."[17] This codification is not so much a *requirement* of institutionality, but a *post facto* consequence of the *phronetic* normativity which *is* constitutive of status functions.[18]

CHAPTER 9

TOPICS CONCERNING INSTITUTIONAL REALITY: REASONS, LANGUAGE, POLITICS, AND THE BACKGROUND

We will briefly consider how the basic account of the creation of institutional facts, as captured in the "X counts as Y in C" formula, intersects with four topics: reasons, language, politics, and the Background. First, Searle's explanation of institutional reality gives us the means to understand Searle's startling contention that there can be desire-independent reasons for action, as found in *Rationality in Action*. This extends his basic account of rational action as found in Chapter 4. Second, Searle contends that language is a kind of institutional fact, but also maintains that language occupies a privileged position with respect to the other institutional facts. We will review and criticize Searle's reasons for his special treatment of language. Third, we will survey a recent essay in which Searle carves out a peculiar functional role for political acts and structures, among the vast variety of institutional facts. Finally, we will consider and criticize the role the Background plays in explaining institutional reality.

DESIRE-INDEPENDENT REASONS FOR ACTION

Recall Searle's account of action. Searle follows Davidson in defining an action as behavior caused by intentional states or reasons, such as beliefs and desires.[1] But Searle goes beyond Davidson in suggesting that while reasons are causally necessary, they are not sufficient for the production of (rational) action. The link between reasons and behavior is mediated by free choice within the gap. Here, an agent, which is sensitive to but not determined by the antecedent reasons, is the more immediate cause of the behavior. Thus, action is distinguished from mere behavior in that action is not just caused by beliefs and desires but is freely chosen. Indeed if a behavior is caused by intentional states, but is not further mediated by volition, it is not a candidate for *rational* action. This is a radical departure from Davidson's Classical Model of action, as freedom seems irreconcilable with Scientific Naturalism.

Having surveyed Searle's account of institutional reality, we are now in the position to articulate another point of difference between Searle's account of action and that of the Classical Model.

According to the Classical Model, every action must include or be proceeded by a set of beliefs and desires. The desires are what Searle calls the "motivator." Every action must include at least one motivator.[2] All motivators specify conditions of satisfaction with an upward, world-to-mind direction of fit; thus, unlike, for example, beliefs, desires in particular and motivators in general represent not how the world in fact is, but how it ought to be.[3] Thus, the reasons which precede the action of raising my arm will include the desire that my arm be raised. Additionally, of course, I may also have the desire to get someone's attention (by means of the raised arm). Both these desires represent conditions of satisfaction (raised arm; caught the attention of a person) with an upward direction of fit.

Searle departs from the Classical Model in holding that, while desires *may* be among an action's motivators, there may also be non-desire-based motivators. That is, where the Classical Model requires that every action be preceded by a desire, Searle denies that all motivators are desires. Searle allows for the possibility of desire-independent motivators or reasons for action.[4]

What are desire-independent reasons for action? They are given by the deontology presupposed by institutional facts. Recall that all status functions distribute rights and obligations to their bearers. Teachers are obliged to instruct in the right way, by grading papers, assigning final grades, lecturing, and so on. Money holders have the right to procure certain commodities. If I am a teacher, and my class has completed a writing assignment, I have a desire-independent reason to grade the papers. I, additionally, may or may not have a *desire* to grade the papers. But even if I do desire to do something else, this does not negate the fact that I also have a desire-independent reason to grade the papers. Likewise, many of the students who wrote the papers may have felt little desire to have done so. For Searle, the fact that they are students—another status function—and that they signed up for the course, is sufficient reason to write a paper. Some of the students may have, additionally, wanted to write the paper or, at least, wanted to avoid the consequences of not writing the paper. While these desires are no doubt helpful, it is important to see that according to Searle's view, even if these desires were not present, there remains a reason to write the paper.

Because institutional reality implicates deontic powers, and these rights and obligations are irreducible to desire-based prudential considerations, institutional players must be capable of being motivated by desire-independent reasons for action. Indeed, given the intimate link between our linguistic competence and institutional reality, Searle contends that language use in general implies the possibility of desire-independent reasons for action. A simple case is that of the commissive or promise. To be able to make a promise already implies the ability to take having done so as a reason for action. If I promise to attend a meeting, my having done so gives me reason for so attending, irrespective of what I in fact want to do.[5] Note that the fact that there are desire-independent reasons does not in any way imply that my desire-independent reasons are never to be overridden by my desires; how the self weighs competing motivators is a separate issue from the more basic contention that there are, in fact, distinct classes of motivators.

Our form of life is permeated with desire-independent rights and obligations, as implied by the institutions within which we act. The actions that are caused by these motivators cannot be exhaustively understood by appeal to prudential or even moral considerations. Institutional reality implies an irreducible domain of reasons for action.

INSTITUTIONAL REALITY, LANGUAGE, AND NORMATIVITY

Language stands in a special relation to the sphere of institutional facts. On the one hand, Searle treats speech acts as one among many kinds of institutional facts. On the other hand, Searle maintains that language underlies all institutional facts; institutional reality is, at its base, language dependent.

As we have seen, in the first half of *The Construction of Social Reality*, Searle distinguishes institutional facts from other kinds of functional facts, including social facts, by appeal to the following criterion: institutional facts, unlike knives, walls, and hearts, perform their function in virtue of something other than their physical features alone.

If institutional facts are simply functional phenomena that bring about ends in a way that is not reliant on the structural-physical features of X alone, then it is easy to see why Searle thinks all cases of language are institutional facts. "Stop!" in certain contexts, serves to inhibit movement. A wall performs an analogous function, but does so in such a way which is reliant on its physical structure. "Stop!" a speech act is an institutional fact, because there is nothing about *this sound* which could so inhibit movement. All instances of language have this conventional quality—there is nothing about the sounds, "Barack Obama is the president of the United States," that makes it represent what it does. Of course a very loud sound might, strictly in virtue of the pain it causes, prevent a hearer from moving closer to the sound and so have the same functional effect that the word "Stop!" might have on English language users. But Searle would contend that the piercing noise is more akin to the wall and is thus neither a speech act nor an institutional fact. It performs its function by virtue of its brute structure alone.

However, the idea that we can identify institutional facts as phenomena that do not perform their function in virtue of their underlying physical structure alone is, as discussed in the last chapter, inadequate. If the sound "Stop!" prohibitively loud, is it *not* a speech act? On Searle's criterion we would be obligated to exclude it from the sphere of the institutional. But surely such a sound is not just startlingly painful but also happens to mean something.

So language, and institutional facts in general, are meaningful by virtue of the second criterion of institutionality—they implicate users in a network of deontic norms. That speech acts *can* do this is easy to see. In promising, I thereby obligate myself to fulfilling the promise. When an officer barks "Stop!" at a soldier, the soldier is obligated to stop. An analogous case is found in Wittgenstein's primitive language, in which a builder prompts his assistant to action by way of various orders ("Block!").[6] But these seem like relatively special cases. If I say "Stop!" to someone who is unwittingly about to walk into oncoming traffic, am I imposing an obligation on them? The case becomes more tricky in thinking about assertives: what right or obligation is implicated when I say, of the world, "Barack Obama is the president of the United States"? What, exactly, is the deontology of a warning, a joke, or a fairy tale?

Nevertheless, Searle seems committed to the view that speech acts have an essential deontological component. A preliminary expression of this view is found in Searle's early paper, "How to Derive an 'Ought' from an 'Is',"[7] wherein he writes:

> It is often a matter of fact that one has certain obligations, commitments, rights, and responsibilities, but it is a matter of institutional, not brute, fact. It is one such institutionalized form of obligation, promising, which I invoked above to derive an "ought" from an "is."[8]

Institutions, including promising, imply rights and obligations.

But in *The Construction of Social Reality* Searle modifies, and in many ways strengthens, the conceptual links between institutional reality, deontology, and language use.

First, where, on Searle's early view, some institutional facts happen to be associated with a norm, he comes to construe deontic power as an essential ingredient of the institutional (i.e., status functions; systems of constitutive rules): in his later work, Searle writes, "all deontic status functions are matters of *conventional power*."[9] In his early paper, Searle makes the weaker claim that only "Some systems of constitutive rules involve obligations, commitments, and responsibilities."[10]

Second, in his later writings Searle claims that *all* speech acts involve obligations, commitments, and responsibilities. If all institutional facts, including speech acts, have a deontic component, then we should expect that other speech acts, besides promises, should be underlain by rights, obligations, and commitments. Indeed, Searle claims precisely this with respect to assertives in *Rationality in Action*.[11] A speaker asserts, "It is raining," which has a downward direction of fit. Searle:

> His utterance now has a status function, it represents, truly or falsely, the state of the weather. And he is not neutral vis-à-vis truth or falsity, because his claim is a claim to truth. *That imposition of that sort of status function, of conditions of satisfaction on conditions of satisfaction, is already a commitment.*[12]

Thus, assertives presuppose an obligation that has an upward direction of fit. Truth, then, is not something that is *added* to an asserted proposition; assertion already implies a commitment to its truth on the part of the speaker. As Searle puts it, "the commitment to truth is internal to statement making."[13] Moreover, Searle also states all speech acts imply a distribution of deontic powers:

> So far we have considered only assertions, but in fact all of the standard forms of speech acts with whole propositional contents involve the creation of desire-independent reasons for action, because the intentional imposition of conditions of satisfaction commits or obligates the speaker in various ways.[14]

Why do speech acts imply obligations and commitments on the part of the speaker? The trivial answer is that speech acts are institutional facts or status functions, and all of the latter are matters of deontic power, so all speech acts implicate rights and obligations. But in *Rationality in Action*, Searle outlines a deeper answer. Why, after all, do all institutional facts, including linguistic facts, implicate deontic powers? Because we *freely and rationally* create institutional facts, including, that is, assertions, by way of the imposition of a status function on some brute X, we are bound to the commitments and obligations implied by such an imposition. In short, "The commitments you undertake are binding on you, because they are your commitments."[15] Perhaps the only reasons for action that an agent can undertake which are absolutely brinding, unconditional, or non-contingent, are those which are freely chosen or endorsed by the actor. This differs from desire dependent reasons for action, whose force depends on whether or not I happen to have the desire in question. If you freely and rationally undertake a game of chess, in some sense bound to move the bishop on the diagonal. Likewise, if you state that something is the case, you, the speaker, cannot remain indifferent to the truth value of my own assertion: "because you freely and intentionally made the assertion and thus committed yourself to its truth, it is not rationally open to you to say that you are indifferent to its truth, or sincerity, or consistency, or evidence, or entailment."[16] Searle thus grounds the normativity implied by institutional facts in his conception of agency, outlined in Chapter 4.

There is a third point of difference between Searle's views in "How to Derive an 'Ought' from an 'Is'" and his latter views. In the early essay Searle does not require that all institutions or systems of constitutive rules are underlain by language itself.

While it is helpful to see illocutionary acts as one among other kinds of institutional facts, Searle, in Chapter 3 of *The Construction of Social Reality*, argues that language in fact underlies all institutional facts—all institutional facts are in fact language dependent. His principle reason for thinking this again depends on the claim that all institutional facts or status functions are underlain by rights and obligations. The deontic structure of institutional reality entails the possibility of remission, wherein the participant violates the obligations imposed on them; this, as we have seen, is distinguishable from failing to perform an assigned function. The diplomat is required, not just to negotiate treaties, but to negotiate them in the right way—within the scope of the deontic powers entailed by the status function of a diplomat. Searle's view is that the capacity to be the bearer of the rights and obligations requires the capacity to represent those rights and obligations to oneself, and this requires language. To see this, recall Searle's example of a tribe's relationship to another tribe's boundary marking, a former wall.

> If our imagined tribe just is not disposed to cross the boundaries as a matter of inclination, they do not in our sense have an institutional fact. They simply have a disposition to behave in certain ways, and their behavior is just like the case of animals marking the limits of their territory. There is nothing deontic about such markings. . . . But if we suppose that the members of the tribe recognize that the line of stones creates rights and obligations, that they are *forbidden* to cross the line, that they are *not supposed to* cross it, then we have symbolization.[17]

The wall does not confer a status onto the members of the tribe because they do not represent either the line of stones or themselves in the right way. Rather, they must represent the line of stones as conferring certain obligations, and they must represent themselves to themselves as bearers of those deontic powers. And this latter capacity requires the ability to use language, which for Searle, is the ability to impose conditions of satisfaction on conditions of satisfaction.

Note that here Searle seems to be claiming that normativity (rights and obligations) require the capacity to represent—an intentional capacity. However, in the discussion of the Background, we will see that Searle locates such norms in the preintentional Background understanding. And because the Background is a presupposition of language, it is not evident that language is in fact necessary for some forms of institutional reality.

Again, while Searle doesn't appear to agree, it seems clear that such tribe members could likewise represent—not just a line of stones—but a wall as conferring deontic powers. Thus, something's institutional status does not in any way appear to depend on whether or not it happens to also perform its function in virtue of its brute structure alone.

INSTITUTIONAL AND POLITICAL REALITY

In his recent essay, "Social Ontology and Political Power,"[18] Searle considers the relationship between institutional reality in general and the state in particular. While political structures are a kind of institution, these structures bear a special relation to the rest of institutional reality.

Governmental or political power is described by Searle as a kind of a superinstitution. This is because governments have the power to regulate many other institutions. Governmental bodies have a disproportionate influence in the determination of what is to count as, e.g. money, citizenship, criminality, private property, marriage, and even language. Because these later nongovernmental institutions are both regulated by political bodies and require collective acceptance constitutive of any institutional fact, the political body itself must typically enjoy an even broader degree of collective acceptance.

How does the government maintain its peculiar status as a steward of institutional reality? On the one hand, it derives its power from the collective and voluntary acceptance of those who fall under its domain. Searle takes this to be the central insight of the social contract theorists, including Thomas Hobbes and John Rawls. On the other hand, a government has the ability to resist dissent by maintaining a monopoly on armed violence. While collective acceptance is necessary for political power, this acceptance is almost always buttressed with an implied threat of violence. However, if a controlling body can enforce a collection of status functions *only* by way of violence, the relation between the occupier and the occupied does not yet count as *political*; to the extent that an unwilling population is acting in accordance with the rights and obligations implied by the status functions; they are acting from prudential rather than desire-independent reasons.

The fact that the political *requires* collective acceptance may be an important point of differentiation between Searle and the social-contract theorists. Where the social-contract theorist contends that collective acceptance, on the model of contractual agreement, is what *legitimates* a political body, Searle makes the stronger claim that collective acceptance is a condition for the possibility of a political relationship in the first place; status functions enforced by force alone are pseudopolitical, desire-dependent or prudential relations.

Searle is aware that the ability to operate by way of voluntary acceptance stands in some tension with the fact that this same body has control over organized violence, and so is in a position to compel acceptance; he calls this the "paradox of government."[19]

Searle's views on political power target those who contend that political power is *simply* a matter of control over the mechanisms of violence. Because political power requires collective acceptance, an organization which distributes status functions does not count as political simply in virtue of the fact that people are acting in accordance with the prescriptions of those status functions. And since political power requires collective acceptance, Searle contends that political power "comes from the bottom up."[20] This, however, is compatible with a characteristic feeling of powerlessness on behalf of those who are subject to a political body's regulatory mechanisms. While in some sense institutional reality is ontologically subjective or socially constructed, and so dependent on us, this does not imply that we each could simply and easily, through an act of will, make it otherwise. Indeed, as Ian Hacking emphasizes in his book *The Social Construction of What?*, part of the force of deeming something "socially constructed" involves overcoming the sense that a status function is somehow unavoidable or inevitable.[21] An important step in changing pernicious conceptions of, for example, gender and race, involves reminding ourselves that alternative conceptions are even possible.

THE BACKGROUND

In both *Intentionality* and *The Social Construction of Reality*, Searle argues that institutional facts, including speech acts, operate within and against a vast, silent "Background" understanding.

Illustrations of How Status Functions and Language Are Underlain by Our Background Understanding

To get a better sense of the Background, consider the following two examples. When a status function (Y) is imposed on a person (X), as when I become a tenant, this implies a distribution of a set of conventional power relations, rights, and obligations. As a tenant, I have the obligation to pay the landlord an agreed-upon rent. I may, depending on the contract, also be obliged to provide a security deposit or pay for utilities. I am also obligated to inform the landlord in advance of my leaving. I have certain rights. I can request that the property is maintained in accordance with the local housing codes. In some states, the landlord is required to return the deposit within three weeks of my moving out (assuming the property is in order and the bills have been paid). In the event of default, I am protected from property confiscation; the landlord may not turn off the utilities or lock me out of the property. Tenancy, thus, is a status function insofar as it implies a bundle of rights and obligations.

But this short list of rights and obligations is only comprehensible to us given a vast Background understanding of how the world in fact works. It presupposes that we know, for example, what a landlord is. A landlord, of course, is another status function that implies its own set of conventional powers. Some of these compliment those of the tenant, so that the landlord has the right to collect monthly rent or the obligation to keep the property up to code. The landlord also has, for example, the obligation to charge tenants within the scope of a city's rent control policies, but perhaps also the right to challenge those very policies in accordance with the laws of that city. A proper understanding of this brief description of tenancy implies much else, most of which goes without saying. It implies a basic understanding of the institution of money and property rights. The very idea of renting makes no sense in a society which has no notion of property or ownership. Tenancy implies that we know that this money is potentially available to a prospective tenant, through employment or other means. It implies an understanding of speech acts, including commissives (making a contract; expressing the intention to leave the property).

But the understanding presupposed by the notion of tenancy isn't limited to the institutional (landlords, property, money, language). The activity of renting only makes sense given the very basic understanding that people are physically vulnerable and so require shelter. Much of this basic understanding consists of truisms so obvious that they rarely merit articulation. If humans were such that we carried our homes on our backs, as turtles do their shells, the very idea that we would pay for shelter might require some explanation. It implies an understanding of human scale. An apartment, advertised as consisting of 1,000 square feet, would nevertheless be unacceptable if the ceiling was found only to be six inches from the floor. Humans are such that we typically live at or near the surface of the earth, so that it is taken for granted that the property is likewise so. It presupposes that humans are the sort of beings who do not drift in and out of existence spontaneously, a fact which if true, might have several implications regarding the calculation of rent. There's no need for the landlord to specify that the property is adequately supplied with oxygen, as this isn't the sort of thing that has to be piped in or otherwise provided, and so on.

The point is, an understanding of tenancy, or any other institutional fact, requires a massive understanding of other institutions, social arrangements, and truisms which flag the kind of beings we are, the sort of activities in which we can and must participate, and the kind of world in which we live. This supplementary understanding, most of which is left unarticulated, constitutes what Searle calls the Background.

The Background also serves to buttress, not just attributions of status, but applications of language. Consider two simple orders: (A) "Cut the grass!" and (B) "Cut the cake!" Intuitively, the word "cut" has the same literal meaning in both (A) and (B). And yet, we interpret these sentences differently. Someone who attempts to cut a cake in the same way that they would cut the grass—as with a lawnmower—will have misunderstood the order. Similarly, someone who attempts to use a knife to divide the grass into a number of equal portions, as they would a cake, will have misunderstood (A). What this shows is that we cannot read the significance of an expression off its literal, dictionary definition.

As in our understanding of the status function of tenant, our understanding of how "cut" functions in the context of various sentences depends on a great deal of Background understanding about how the world works. Given that cake is for eating, the kind of cuts a lawnmower would make in it undermines the role it plays in our activities. This, of course, presupposes much: cake is the sort of thing which is big enough to require division, humans are the sort of beings that need to eat, cake does not grow, the mouth with which people eat is of limited size, and so on. Likewise, for cutting grass. These presuppositions almost never need to be stated, unless we are, perhaps, teaching the word "cut" to a small child (or having a discussion about the nature of Background presuppositions). But even in that case we would not point out that objects of certain kinds of material more easily penetrate other kinds of material or even that objects extended in space are, at least in principle, divisible. Searle claims that even though we *could* say such things, we could not articulate *everything* that constitutes our general understanding of how things work. This understanding is largely in our bones, not in our head.

What is the Background?

The Background falls within a family of concepts posited by, among others, Wittgenstein (form of life), Heidegger (das Man), and Bourdieu (habitus). It is comprised of an open fabric of expectations against which we understand, i.e., the literal meaning of a sentence or the rights and obligations implied by a given status function. But these are just two examples of how the Background structures our understanding. The Background is pervasive: it conditions our perception (so that we see certain collections of wood as tables), it brings events under a narrative structure, it allows us to screen certain events as relevant or irrelevant, and it structures our consciousness (bringing events and experiences under the aspect of familiarity).[22]

Because the Background underlies our understanding, it is tempting to think of it as a collection of very basic beliefs. I know that the lawn is to be cut with a mower and not a knife because I *believe* that lawn grows, that it is found on large, flat surfaces of soil, and so on. I know that the landlord is to keep the property up to code because I already believe that landlords own the property in question, and that there are certain statutes which require owners to keep the property within the scope of the code, and so on. But while parts of the Background can be articulated and so formulated in terms of beliefs, the Background is not itself constituted by these beliefs.

The ancient Greek philosophers distinguished between two kinds of knowledge. *Epistêmê* is theoretical knowledge consisting of beliefs, propositions, or theories, which represent the world under one aspect or another. *Epistêmê* is explicit and intentional, having representational content or conditions of satisfaction. When we *say* or *believe* that grass is a low, nonwoody plant which tends to grow in sprawling patches, this is *epistêmê*. *Technê* is typically translated as craft, skill, or know-how and constitutes a second variety of knowledge. *Technê* captures the sense in which I know how to ride a bike or work a clutch. I might be perfectly competent at such activities but find myself at a loss if prompted to explain or articulate how I do such things. Children learn how to speak grammatically *before* they are taught to bring those skills under the various grammatical categories—noun, verb, preposition, and so on. For Searle, the Background knowledge is *technê* or know-how. It is in our bones. Of course it can, at least in part, be articulated and so translated into *epistêmê*. But this fact should not mislead us into thinking that our Background understanding is a matter of *epistêmê* in the first place.

Searle is explicit about the status of the Background. In *Intentionality* he writes,

> The Background is a set of nonrepresentational mental capacities that enable all representing to take place. Intentional states only have the conditions of satisfaction that they do, and thus only are the states that they are, against a Background of abilities that are not themselves Intentional states.[23]

Epistêmê or representational knowledge is thus founded on nonrepresentational, nonintentional sets of dispositions, capacities, or know-how.

A Problem with the Notion of the Background

The Background appears to have no place in Searle's basic ontology. According to Searle's Scientific Naturalism, this ontology is roughly the world as described by physics. These brute facts are organized into systems which are defined in terms of what they do, their causal relations. Some higher-level systems are organisms and some of these acquire nervous systems, the causal basis for intentional consciousness.

In a world that consists exclusively of particles in fields of force, various orders of systems including organisms, and intentionality, there seems little or no room for the Background. If the Background were intentional—and so a kind of *epistêmê*—then the task of explaining what it is, and how it is compatible with Searle's physicalist ontology, can be collapsed into the mind-body problem. One may worry whether Searle's solution to the mind-body problem is adequate, but at least Searle isn't saddled with an *additional* philosophical problem (the Background-body problem). The difficulty, of course, is that by Searle's own admission, the Background structures intentionality; that is, intentionality presupposes the Background. Or, more generally, *epistêmê* presupposes *technê*, so that the latter can't be collapsed into the former. Thus in addition to showing how intentionality is possible within a world consisting of nothing but particles in fields of force, Searle has to show how, further, the Background itself is compatible with Scientific Naturalism.

In *Intentionality* Searle simply says that while the Background is *akin* to intentional representations (*epistêmê*), it is not intentional. Searle is aware of the tendency to talk about the Background misleadingly, in terms of *epistêmê*.

> Ordinary usage invites us to, and we can and do, treat elements of the Background as if they were representations, but it does not follow from that, nor is it the case that, when these elements are functioning they function as representations.[24]

Thus, Searle prefers to talk about the Background, less in terms of assumptions, presuppositions, or expectations but rather in terms of dispositions or capacities, which are less suggestive of intentionality.

But what or *where* is the Background, if not in the mind? If the Background is not ontologically subjective, then perhaps it is ontologically objective.

Twelve years later, in *The Construction of Social Reality*, Searle answers this question: "It is important to see that when we talk about the Background we are talking about a certain category of neurophysiological causation."[25] It is easy to understand why Searle is driven to this view: if the Background is not to be found in the mind (intentionality), then naturally it must be in the body. But this suggestion is untenable. The problem, in short, is that while the Background is nonintentional, it still implies a degree of normativity. If Searle collapses the Background into neurophysiological causation, he collapses "ought" into "is," and strips the Background of its normativity.

By way of elaboration, skills or *epistêmê* always imply the possibility of failure (and expertise). I can fail to ride a bike or use the clutch when shifting gears. There is something wrong with the person who speaks ungrammatically, doesn't know that the landlord is also the owner of the property (and so subject to certain obligations), or who fails to understand that grass is the sort of thing that is cut with a mower and not a knife. To say that our experience is structured against a Background know-how must imply that we in some sense *ought* to have that understanding.

Searle is not silent on the question of how normativity is possible in a world consisting entirely of particles in fields of force. Indeed, Searle seems to recognize this difficulty, although he articulates it in terms of rule-following. Rule-following—that is, normativity—is most easily understood intentionalistically, as when I *decide* not to drive faster than the speed limit and so on.

> If we think of the Background intentionalistically, then we have abandoned the thesis of the Background. . . . But if, on the other hand, we say that the rules play no causal role at all in the behavior, then we must say that the Background is such that this is just what the person does, he just behaves that way.[26]

Searle rejects both views as unacceptable. So, here, he appears to recognize that *if* the Background is *just* a category of neurophysiological causation, this is tantamount to stripping it of the normativity which is otherwise implied when it is paraphrased in terms of explicit rules or intentionality. He is not, however, entirely explicit about this.

Understanding Searle's positive view about the status of the Background is tricky, partially because the above quotation comes up in the context of a different, although related, puzzle. Searle, thus, only indirectly tackles the question of how a normativity-laden Background is compatible with his basic scientific ontology.

It is worth pursuing these matters in greater detail.

The question we have been pursuing is how the normativity of the Background is possible. The easiest way to construe normativity is in terms of intentional rule-following (rights and obligations). But Searle argues that the Background is preintentional, and so cannot be brought under this picture of norms. But, if we grant that the Background is just a "category of neurophysiological causation," then this appears to strip it of all normativity: the Background, in this view, is "just what a person does." But Searle rejects this view out of hand. The latter view, moreover, defies the sense in which the Background is a kind of know-how.

Can Searle's various, seemingly incompatible articulations of the Background be brought together again?

As mentioned, the view that the Background cannot be understood behavioristically, as "just what the person does," comes up in the context of an another question. Institutions, as we have seen, have a conventional power structure and are underlain by a system of rules in the form of rights and obligations. As a tenant, I am obliged to pay the landlord rent. What, Searle asks, explains this normativity-laden behavior? Sometimes we consciously or even subconsciously *follow* rules, so that we can explain a subset of this behavior by appeal to intentionality. Thus, as a tenant, I might *reflect* on the fact that I have this obligation which prompts me to send the check. I thus intentionally follow the rules implied by being a tenant. But typically, in paying my rent, I just do it. I do not remember reflecting on the rule or even deciding to pay my rent. Of course, if my landlord dramatically increases my rent, I might then consciously decide to pay the rent (or decide not to) but this is not the typical case. So what, if not intentionality, accounts for my acting in accordance with the rules?

At this point it is helpful to draw attention to an asymmetry in the role the Background plays in explaining intentionality (a mental fact) as opposed to the role it plays in explaining status functions (an institutional fact). In *Intentionality*, Searle explains intentional representation (*epistêmê*) by appealing to nonintentional know-how (*technê*), which is somehow explained by appeal to brute configurations of blind causation. But in *The Construction of Social Reality* Searle does not attempt to explain status functions per se, so much as normativity-laden behavior (paying the rent). So what explains this behavior? Now given the role that the Background plays in *Intentionality*, one would expect Searle just to appeal to the Background or know-how which anyway explains intentionality. But he doesn't.

He cannot do this because, somewhere along the line, he *identifies* the normativity-laden behavior (paying the rent) *with* the know-how or Background which could otherwise be used to explain it! The baseball player "acquires a set of Background habits, skills, dispositions that are such that when he hits the ball, he runs to first base."[27] The tenant acquires a set of behaviors, such that the rent is paid. Thus, a potential explanans becomes the explanandum.

This identification is puzzling for other reasons—how is running to first base or paying rent a "category of neurophysiological causation"? In any case, he is now in the awkward position of explaining, not just why the baseball player runs to first base or why the tenant pays rent, but the Background itself. First-base running or rent-paying behavior becomes a stand-in for all varieties of know-how. Searle doesn't explain rule-following behavior by appeal to the Background, as he explains intentionality or literal utterances; he has to explain the Background itself.

So if first-base running or rent-paying behavior is a stand-in for know-how in general, and know-how is normative (rule-following), what explains this Background? More specifically, how is the normativity which is indicative of the Background possible? Obviously he can't appeal to intentional representation, as the Background is a condition for its possibility. Another way of putting this is that we can't explain *techné* by appeal to *epistémé*. But, as we have seen, he can't appeal to blind, brute facts in explanation of the normativity either. The appeal to behaviorism in this context would not *explain* how know-how is possible; it's a *rejection* of the question, in that it contends that the question's topic is false (there is no normativity laden know-how; there is just brute behavior).[28]

What, then, explains the normativity indicative of the Background-as-*techné*? Searle's answer: "we evolve a set of dispositions that are sensitive to the rule structure."[29] That is, we explain our know-how (Background, paying the rent without thinking about it), which is normative, by appeal to the rules: we develop "a set of dispositions that are sensitive and responsive to the specific content of those rules."[30] In the following passage note the way in which the Background, as dispositions or know-how, gets *identified* with the behavior under investigation:

> The users of money do not know those rules, and in general, I am arguing, they do not apply them consciously or unconsciously; rather, they have developed a set of dispositions that are sensitive and responsive to the specific content of those rules. . . . And those sorts of abilities, this type of know-how, that become ingrained are in fact a reflection of the sets of constitutive rules whereby we impose functions on entities that do not have those functions in virtue of their physical structure, but acquire the function only through collective agreement or acceptance.[31]

We are accountable for the behavior (dispositions, capacities), not because we intended to follow a set of rules and not because the behavior is somehow grounded in blind causation, but because it is sensitive to some sort of rule structure.

The natural question is, of course, what or where is this rule structure to which Searle is helping himself? It obviously can't be the Background, because this is what he is trying to explain. Nor can it be intentional, as he explicitly rejects that hypothesis. Searle leaves *this* question unanswered.[32] It looks as though Searle has to include *rules* within his basic ontology if he is going to account for the know-how which is indicative of our institutionally significant behavior. But this suggestion is at odds with the initial characterization of the project, wherein he promises to answer the following question: If "institutional facts exist only within systems of constitutive rules," then "how do we make the connection between the fundamental ontology of conscious biological beasts like ourselves and the apparatus of social facts and human institutions?"[33]

NOTES

INTRODUCTION

[1] David Papineau, "Power and Consciousness on the Clapham Omnibus," *Times Online* (2008), http://entertainment.timesonline.co.uk/tol/arts_and_entertainment/the_tls/article3196720.ece.

[2] John R. Searle, *Intentionality* (Cambridge: Cambridge University Press, 1983), x.

[3] In a recent essay, Searle outlines a chain of ontological dependency that begins with brute facts and ends with politics and ethics, proceeding through mind, language, rationality, and institutionality. This ontological hierarchy implies a natural sequence of philosophical investigation. John R. Searle, "What Is to Be Done?" *Topoi* 25 (2006): 104. John R. Searle, *Freedom and Neurobiology: Reflections on Free Will, Language, and Political Power*, Columbia Themes in Philosophy (New York: Columbia University Press, 2007), 15–16.

[4] This formulation of Searle's philosophical agenda, which sees philosophy as reconciling human experience with science, may in fact not be limited to the latter part of his career. As Searle has recently claimed, "It took me a long time to realize that, though I had not been aware of it, [this] agenda . . . had always been my agenda." Contrariwise, David Papineau distinguishes between an early and later Searle: "Over the years Searle has drifted away from his Oxford roots." Where the later Searle is preoccupied with the task of explaining how humans fit into the world as described by science, the early Searle works within the scope of the Oxford ordinary language tradition. Searle, "What Is to Be Done?" 101. Papineau, "Power and Consciousness on the Clapham Omnibus."

CHAPTER 1: FUNDAMENTAL ONTOLOGY: EXTERNAL REALISM AND SCIENTIFIC NATURALISM

[1] M. W. Barsoum, A. Ganguly, and G. Hug, "Microstructural Evidence of Reconstituted Limestone Blocks in the Great Pyramids of Egypt," *Journal of the American Ceramic Society* 89, no. 12 (2006): 3788–96.

[2] Such a background theory can constitute the *contrast-class*, a condition for the possibility of a why-question's arising. Bas C. van Fraassen,

The Scientific Image (Oxford; New York: Clarendon Press; Oxford University Press, 1980), 141–42.

3 John R. Searle, *The Construction of Social Reality* (New York: The Free Press, 1995), xi.

4 George Berkeley, *A Treatise Concerning the Principles of Human Knowledge* (Oxford; New York: Oxford University Press, 1998), §6.

5 It should be noted that where Berkeley denies the existence of a representation-independent world, Russell's attitude is that of the agnostic. "It is possible that there may be all these things that the physicalist talks about in actual reality, but it is impossible that we should ever have any reason whatsoever for supposing that there are." Searle's External Realism positively affirms that of which Russell is cautiously skeptical. See Bertrand Russell, *The Philosophy of Logical Atomism*, ed. David Francis Pears (LaSalle, Ill.: Open Court, 1985), 144. Indeed, in other writings, Russell deploys an inference to the best-explanation-type argument to contend that the existence of a representation-independent world isn't only possible, but likely. See Bertrand Russell, *The Problems of Philosophy* (Mineola, New York: Dover Publications, 1999).

6 John R. Searle, "Toward a Unified Theory of Reality," *Harvard Review of Philosophy* 12 (2004): 97.

7 See Searle, *The Construction of Social Reality*, Chapters 7 and 8.

8 Ibid., 187–88.

9 Robert Hanna, in offering an interpretation of the Refutation of Idealism, suggests several senses in which objects may be said to be "external," the strongest of which is that it is mind-independent. Kant endorses a weaker version of externality than does Searle. Robert Hanna, *Kant, Science, and Human Nature* (Oxford; New York: Clarendon Press; Oxford University Press, 2006), 69.

10 G. E. Moore, "Proof of an External World," in *Philosophical Papers* (London; New York: Allen & Unwin; Macmillan, 1959).

11 Searle, *The Construction of Social Reality*, 177–82.

12 Ludwig Wittgenstein, *On Certainty*, trans. G. E. M. Anscombe and G. H. von Wright (New York: Harper, 1969).

13 Note that the label "Scientific Naturalism" is not Searle's own.

14 Searle, *The Construction of Social Reality*, 5–7.

15 Ibid., 6.

16 This assessment and the following historical review owe much to Robert Hanna's book, *Kant, Science, and Human Nature*. Hanna, in turn, is tracing the surveys of Hilary Putnam and John McDowell. Hanna, *Kant, Science, and Human Nature*, 8.

17 Wilfrid Sellars, *Philosophy and the Scientific Image of Man*, ed. Robert Garland Colodny, Frontiers of Science and Philosophy (Pittsburgh, Pa.: University of Pittsburgh Press, 1962), 35–78.

18 Frank Jackson, *From Metaphysics to Ethics: A Defence of Conceptual Analysis* (Oxford; New York: Clarendon Press; Oxford University Press, 1998), 5.

19 Searle, "What Is to Be Done?" 101.

20 Searle, "Toward a Unified Theory of Reality," 107.

21 Searle, "What Is to Be Done?" 101. Searle, *Freedom and Neurobiology*, 4.

22 In some ways, Hacking's label is preferable. "Realism" seems to be a claim about what exists (i.e., the objects of science) rather than a claim about the nature of the relation between concepts and the world. Ian Hacking, *The Social Construction of What?* (Cambridge, Mass.: Harvard University Press, 1999), 83.

23 Hilary Putnam, "Why There Isn't a Ready-Made World," *Synthese* 51, no. 2 (1982): 142.

24 Thomas S. Kuhn, *Structure of Scientific Revolutions*, 3rd ed. (Chicago, Ill.: The University of Chicago Press, 1962).

25 Nelson Goodman, *Of Mind and Other Matters* (Cambridge, Mass.: Harvard University Press, 1984).

26 Searle, *The Construction of Social Reality*, 160.

27 Ibid., 155.

28 Andrew Pickering, *Constructing Quarks: A Sociological History of Particle Physics* (Chicago, Ill.: University of Chicago Press, 1984).

CHAPTER 2: CONSCIOUSNESS AND MATERIALIST THEORIES OF THE MIND

1 John R. Searle, *The Rediscovery of the Mind* (Cambridge, Mass.: MIT Press, 1992), 63.

2 Paul Feyerabend, "Mental Events and the Brain," *Journal of Philosophy* 40 (1963). R. Rorty, "Mind-Body Identity, Privacy and Categories," *Review of Metaphysics* 19, no. 1 (1965).

3 U. T. Place, "Is Consciousness a Brain Process?" *British Journal of Psychology* 47 (1956). J. J. C. Smart, "Sensations and Brain Processes," *The Philosophical Review* 68, no. 2 (1959).

4 Searle, *The Rediscovery of the Mind*, 52.

5 Ibid., 84.

6 T. Nagel, "What is it Like to Be a Bat?" *The Philosophical Review* 83, no. 4 (1974).

7 Frank Jackson, "What Mary Didn't Know," *The Journal of Philosophy* 83, no. 5 (1986).

8 Searle, *The Rediscovery of the Mind*, 65–70.

9 Ibid., 70–71.

10 John R. Searle, "The Chinese Room," in *The MIT Encyclopedia of the Cognitive Sciences*, ed. R. A. Wilson and F. Keil (Cambridge, Mass.: MIT Press, 1999).

11 Alan M. Turing, "Computing Machinery and Intelligence," *Mind*, no. 54 (1950).

12 David Pitt, "Mental Representation," in *The Stanford Encyclopedia of Philosophy*, ed. Edward N. Zalta (2008).

13 Searle, *The Rediscovery of the Mind*, Chapter 7.

14 The unconscious is, for Nietzsche, a network of "causal relations which are entirely withheld from us." Friedrich Wilhelm Nietzsche, *The Will to*

Power, ed. Walter Arnold Kaufmann and R. J. Hollingdale (New York: Random House, 1967).

[15] Advocates of the causal-information theory of mind include Fred Dretski, Jerry Fodor, and Michael Devitt.

[16] Searle, *The Rediscovery of the Mind*, xii.

[17] Ibid., 1.

[18] Note that while materialists might endorse the analogies offered, they may still disagree with the "caused by/feature of" characterization of those phenomena.

[19] The claim that the mental is both caused by and a feature of the underlying neurophysiology is more compelling as an argument to the effect that higher-level phenomena, such as inflation or consciousness, are not causally inert. But this claim more directly concerns the possibility of intentional causation than a resolution to the traditional mind-body problem (see Chapter 4). Indeed this may be already to presuppose, against the materialist, that the mental is a higher-order system and, further, that this higher-order system has the qualitative subjectivity indicative of conscious states. To argue for these latter claims, Searle must rely on his Silicon Brains and Conscious Robots arguments. Unfortunately, these arguments drive such a deep conceptual wedge between the mind and brain (behavior, broadly construed) that it is difficult to see the sense in which the mind could still be held to be a feature realized in the brain.

[20] John R. Searle, *Mind: A Brief Introduction* (Oxford; New York: Oxford University Press, 2004), 116.

[21] Van Fraassen, *The Scientific Image*, 141–42.

[22] John R. Searle, *Mind, Language, and Society: Philosophy in the Real World* (New York: Basic Books, 1998), 54.

CHAPTER 3: INTENTIONAL MENTAL STATES

[1] So far as the ontology of models go, contemporary theorists are reluctant to identify models with either linguistic or pictorial entities. In Roman Frigg's view, descriptions describe models, which is a structural, imagined entity. If this is the case, then the intentional content of an intentional state might be helpfully *identified* with a model. See Roman Frigg, "Re-Presenting Scientific Representation," *Dissertation* (2003) (Unpublished).

[2] Searle, *Intentionality*, 11–12.

[3] See "Meaning, Communication, and Representation" for an extensive discussion of the way that mental representation is both like and unlike models and forms of pictorial representation. John R. Searle, "Meaning, Communication, and Representation," in *Philosophical Grounds of Rationality: Intentions, Categories, Ends*, ed. Richard E. Grandy and Richard Warner (Oxford: Clarendon Press, 1986).

[4] Searle agrees with Wittgenstein's rejection of the idea that mental states refer in virtue of their being pictures in the head. "If the meaning of the sign (roughly, that which is of importance about the sign) is an image built

up in our minds when we see or hear the sign, then first let us adopt the method we just described of replacing this mental image by some outward object seen, e.g. a painted or modeled image. Then why should the written sign plus this painted image be alive if the written sign alone was dead?" See Ludwig Wittgenstein, *Blue and Brown Books* (New York: Perennial, 1942), 4–5. Searle points out that pictures (or sentences) are *used* in a way that mental states are not, and so require an agent (a user)—we can, in the case of the former, distinguish the underlying brute fact from its content. But this distinction makes no sense in the case of mental states themselves; there is nothing more to a mental state besides its counterfactual content. The analogy between models and mental states is not meant to suggest an explanation of *how* intentional states refer. Nevertheless, the comparison is useful in clarifying some of the logical properties of intentional states. See Searle's response to Dennett in Searle, *Intentionality*, 21–22.

5   This way of talking about the content of representational states can be traced to Saul Kripke and, more recently, Robert Stalnaker. Following Stalnaker, talk of possible worlds should not imply an implausible metaphysics. Robert Stalnaker, "Assertion," in *Context and Content: Essays on Intentionality in Speech and Thought* (Oxford; New York: Oxford University Press, 1999), 79.

6   This suggestion finds its roots in Kant. Immanuel Kant, *Critique of Pure Reason*, trans. Paul Guyer and Allen W. Wood (Cambridge; New York: Cambridge University Press, 1998), A239/B98.

7   This discussion owes much to Michael Shaffer's discussion of idealization in modeling. Michael J. Shaffer, "Bayesian Confirmation of Theories that Incorporate Idealizations," *Philosophy of Science* 68, no. 3 (2001): 41–42.

8   This is a complicated issue. A model typically aims to represent the world as it is, so that Marx attempts to represent social development in terms of production, culminating in communism. In the event of a discrepancy between the possible world represented by Marx and the actual world, the fault lies with Marx's belief or model. Lenin, on the other hand, took the content as a prescription rather than as (simply) a description, and endeavored to change the world so as to bring it into alignment with the conditions of satisfaction. According to Lenin's psychological mode, that same model or content has a world-to-mind direction of fit. There is also a more subtle way in which a scientific model does not function simply to represent the world as it is. This model may, further, function as a Kuhnian paradigm if it is upheld as an exemplar of model making. Theorists, working in related fields, endeavor to make their models more like the paradigm case. In this case, the paradigm doesn't just represent the world, but might be said to serve as a kind of object of desire with a world-to-mind direction of fit. Scientists endeavor to make their extant theories more like the paradigm case so that the latter serves as a condition of satisfaction (requirement). See Kuhn, *Structure of Scientific Revolutions*.

9   Searle, *Intentionality*, 7.

[10] Ibid., 177.
[11] Ibid., 13.
[12] Ibid., 29–36.
[13] Ibid., 36.
[14] Beliefs must, however, be potentially conscious. See the discussion of Searle's connection principle in Chapter 2.
[15] Searle, *Intentionality*, 47.

CHAPTER 4: REASON AND ACTION

[1] Searle, *Intentionality*, 16, 87. Wittgenstein's original quotation can be found in Ludwig Wittgenstein, *Philosophical Investigations*, trans. G. E. M. Anscombe, 3rd ed. (New Jersey: Prentice-Hall, 1958), §612.
[2] Donald Davidson, "Actions, Reasons, and Causes," in *Essays on Actions and Events* (Oxford; New York: Clarendon Press; Oxford University Press, 2001), 9.
[3] Ibid.
[4] The following discussion, along with a few of its examples, is more or less derived from Larry Wright, *Critical Thinking* (Oxford: Oxford University Press, 2001).
[5] "Because$_e$" also includes functional explanation.
[6] Wright, *Critical Thinking*, 62.
[7] Davidson, "Actions, Reasons, and Causes," 11.
[8] This behavior could plausibly still be construed as an action, if the man told us that he flailed in order to get the spider web off of him. But merely purposive, goal-directed behaviors—which we might equally attribute to the spider that spun the web—are not paradigm cases of intentional, autonomous, self-conscious, agentive action. The line between action and body movements that are not actions, is continuous; while waving someone down falls on one end of the continuum, reacting to an unseen cobweb tends toward the other. See Harry G. Frankfurt, *The Importance of What We Care About: Philosophical Essays* (Cambridge [England] ; New York: Cambridge University Press, 1988).
[9] This example is found in Wright, *Critical Thinking*, 158–59.
[10] G. E. M. Anscombe, *Intention* (Ithaca, N.Y.: Cornell University Press, 1957), 18.
[11] Davidson, "Actions, Reasons, and Causes," 11.
[12] John R. Searle, *Rationality in Action* (Cambridge, Mass.: MIT Press, 2001), 118–19.
[13] Donald Davidson, "Intending," in *Essays on Actions and Events* (Oxford; New York: Clarendon Press; Oxford University Press, 2001).
[14] Searle, *Intentionality*, 84–85.
[15] R. M. Chisholm, "Freedom in Action," in *Freedom and Determinism*, ed. Keith Lehrer (New York: Random House, 1966), 37. See an analogous example in Donald Davidson, "Freedom to Act," in *Essays on Freedom of Action*, ed. Ted Honderich (London; Boston: Routledge and Kegan Paul, 1973), 33–34.

16 Note that the apparatus developed in *Rationality in Action*, discussed below, affords Searle a more elegant solution to the deviant causal chain problem. The difference between murdering and accidentally killing someone (in spite of having the intention to do so) is that, in the former case, the agent willed or chose to kill. This is not the same as having an operative intention or reason to kill. Reasons don't kill, selves do (for reasons).

17 Searle might grant the possibility of genuine indeterminacy, as on the quantum level.

18 Searle, *Rationality in Action*, 62.

19 Note that there seem to be other places where freedom might intervene. We are not, for example, passive recipients of an intentional store. There is a gap between our perceptual experiences and the beliefs we infer from them. Perceptual experiences can underdetermine the latter. At least to the extent that this is the case, we have a degree of control over which beliefs we will endorse. Similar remarks can be made about hierarchies of desire.

20 Searle, *Rationality in Action*, 12–13.

21 Ibid., 5.

22 Ibid., 297.

23 Ibid.

CHAPTER 5: FROM ACTS TO SPEECH ACTS: THE INTENTION TO COMMUNICATE

1 John R. Searle, *Speech Acts* (Cambridge: Cambridge University Press, 1969), 16.

2 Reading *Speech Acts* back through the lens of *Rationality in Action*, Searle might also add that a dog which happens to make the sound "hello" is not using language precisely because the utterance, while an action, is not a rational action.

3 Searle, *Speech Acts*, 3.

4 P. F. Strawson, "Meaning and Truth," in *Logico-Linguistic Papers* (London: Methuen, 1971).

5 Ibid., 176.

6 Ludwig Wittgenstein, *Tractatus Logico-Philosophicus*, ed. David Francis Pears and Brian McGuinness, Routledge Classics (London; New York: Routledge, 2001), 2.12.

7 Ibid., 2.1511.

8 Wittgenstein, *Philosophical Investigations*, I.23.

9 Ibid., I.11.

10 Strawson, "Meaning and Truth," 173.

11 John R. Searle, "A Philosophical Self-Portrait," in *The Penguin Dictionary of Philosophy*, ed. Thomas Mautner (London; New York: Penguin Books, 1997), 512.

12 Searle, *Speech Acts*, 43.

13 Ibid., 17.

[14] Ibid., 43.

[15] Searle, "Meaning, Communication, and Representation," 109–10.

[16] H. P. Grice, "Meaning," *The Philosophical Review* 66, no. 3 (1957): 217.

[17] Searle, *Speech Acts*, 37.

[18] H. P. Grice, *Studies in the Way of Words* (Cambridge, Mass.: Harvard University Press, 1989), 109, 218.

[19] It is, perhaps, an open question as to whether Bill *meant* that he couldn't play squash in showing his bandaged leg.

[20] Christine Kenneally, *The First Word: The Search for the Origins of Language* (New York: Viking, 2007), 127.

[21] Searle grants that even some illocutionary effects can be brought about in a nonconventional way. Searle, *Speech Acts*, 38. There are, however, a number of passages in *The Construction of Social Reality*, where Searle holds that institutional facts cannot perform their function in virtue of their physical structure alone, which would suggest that Searle has retracted this qualification.

CHAPTER 6: FROM SOUNDS TO WORDS: THE INTENTION TO REPRESENT

[1] Searle and Austin have differing conceptions of the illocutionary act. For Austin, the distinction between the locutionary and illocutionary can be elucidated in terms of content and force. What is the basis by which the content is separated from the force? Philosophers of language have been impressed by the fact that several different speech acts can nevertheless have a shared content, as when I say "The car is washed," "Wash the car!" or "I promise to wash the car." In asking someone to wash the car, I represent a world in which the car is washed and then bring that content under a certain force. The locutionary act proffers a certain content, whereas the illocutionary act brings that locution under a certain force—an assertion, order, or promise. Note that, for Searle, the linguistic distinction between content and force is analogous to the structure of intentional states, where a representative content can be brought under different psychological modes or forces. This is not accidental. As we will see, the distinction between an expression's illocutionary force and propositional content is dependent on and explained by the mind's capacity for intentionality. Austin and Searle stress different features of the illocutionary act. For Searle the essence of the illocutionary act is found in the Gricean intentions to communicate. But Austin takes it for granted that the speaker is communicating, and emphasizes the fact that illocutionary acts can bring certain content under a variety of different psychological modes or forces. For Searle, this function is achieved by the intention to represent, which is, as we will see, part of the total illocutionary act.

[2] J. L. Austin, *How to Do Things with Words*, The William James Lectures; 1955 (Cambridge, Mass.: Harvard University Press, 1962), 95.

[3] Ibid.

[4] Ibid.

[5] Austin would probably be reluctant to grant that the various acts are individuated and caused by a characteristic sets of underlying intentions; this interpretation is a product of Searle's imposition of a Davidsonian account of action onto Austin's taxonomy of speech actions.

[6] Kent Bach, "Speech Acts and Pragmatics," in *The Blackwell Guide to the Philosophy of Language*, ed. Michael Devitt and Richard Hanley (Malden, Mass.: Blackwell Pub., 2006), 149–50.

[7] Indeed, in Chapter 7, I will argue, against Searle, that there is a sense in which an officer who says "show your passport" but does not also have the functional, perlocutionary intention cannot be said to *mean* what they said.

[8] Grice, "Meaning."

[9] Stephen R. Schiffer, *Meaning* (Oxford: Clarendon Press, 1972).

[10] Stalnaker, "Assertion," 87.

[11] Searle, *Speech Acts*, 46.

[12] Stalnaker makes a similar response against an analogous objection, where the "essential effect" is not unfairly characterized as something like a perlocutionary effect. "My suggestion about the essential effect of assertion does not imply that speakers intend to succeed in getting the addressee to accept the content of the assertion, or that they believe they will, or even might succeed. A person may make an assertion knowing it will be rejected just as Congress may pass a law knowing it will be vetoed, a labor negotiator may make a proposal knowing it will be met by a counterproposal, or a poker player may place a bet knowing it will cause all the other players to fold." Stalnaker, "Assertion," 87.

[13] Searle, *Speech Acts*, 43.

[14] In his later writings, Searle suggests that these three intentions are in fact three aspects of one complex intention. Searle, *Mind, Language, and Society*, 141–44.

[15] Searle, *Intentionality*, 167–68.

[16] Searle, *Speech Acts*, 64, 60; Searle, *Intentionality*, 174–75.

[17] Searle, *Intentionality*, 167.

[18] Searle, *Speech Acts*, 64, 60.

[19] The work of this third intention is actually accomplished by two intentions for Austin: the rhetic intention imposes conditions of satisfaction on the behavior, sound, and marks. The illocutionary intention then imposes a force on those same brute facts. Searle reserves the notion of the illocutionary intention for the intention to communicate by conventional means, and posits an additional intention—the intention to represent—to do the work of the intentional imposition.

[20] Dreyfus writes, "According to Searle, the intention in action is the experience of acting—what William James calls 'the feeling of effort.' . . . On Searle's analysis, all acting is accompanied by an experience of acting, and this experience of effort has as its intentional content that it is causing my body movements." Hubert L. Dreyfus, *Being-in-the-World: A Commentary on Heidegger's Being and Time, Division I* (Cambridge, Mass.: MIT Press, 1991), 56.

[21] Grice, "Meaning," 386.

22 Searle responds that ". . . Dreyfus is so wedded to phenomenology that he literally is unable to see that I am not doing phenomenology. I am engaged, among other things, in logical analysis and that enterprise is quite different from phenomenology." John R. Searle, "The Limits of Phenomenology," in *Essays in Honor of Hubert L. Dreyfus*, ed. Hubert L. Dreyfus, Mark A. Wrathall, and J. E. Malpas (Cambridge, Mass.: MIT Press, 2000), 74–75.

23 John R. Searle, "A Taxonomy of Illocutionary Acts," in *Expression and Meaning: Studies in the Theory of Speech Acts* (Cambridge; New York: Cambridge University Press, 1979).

24 John R. Searle, "How Performatives Work," *Linguistics and Philosophy* 12 (1989).

CHAPTER 7: ON THE MEANING OF MEANING: CRITICAL REMARKS

1 Searle, "Meaning, Communication, and Representation," 212.

2 Ibid., 218.

3 Ibid., 216.

4 Ibid., 210.

5 Indeed, the causal chains of dependency are considerably more complicated than this. Any functional or justificatory chain already implies a larger causal chain which tracks those relations. See Larry Wright, *Teleological Explanations: An Etiological Analysis of Goals and Functions* (Berkeley, Calif.: University of California Press, 1976).

6 Austin, *How to Do Things with Words*, 146.

7 William Ramsey, "Prototypes and Conceptual Analysis," in *Rethinking Intuition: The Psychology of Intuition and Its Role in Philosophical Inquiry*, ed. Michael R. DePaul and William Ramsey (Lanham, Md.: Rowman & Littlefield, 1998).

8 A speaker makes an assertion with the intention that saying so will move the hearer to believe that it is so; sometimes, as in philosophy, I make an assertion but expect the hearer to believe for reasons independent of my saying so. Austin was characteristically sensitive to these differences and suggested that there are in fact two different categories of assertion: (1) *verdictives* are assertions whose truth are supported by reasons; (2) *expositives* are assertions not buttressed by explicit reasons; the fact that the speaker is asserting something is typically reason, depending on the context, to believe its truth. Searle is dissatisfied with this distinction, or else fails to see its motivation, and reduces the categories of the verdictive and the expositive to the assertive: "This class will contain most of Austin's expositives and many of his verdictives as well for the, by now I hope obvious, reason that they all have the same illocutionary point and differ only in other features of illocutionary force." Having done this, he then fails to see the ordinary cases in which asserting alone constitutes a reason for a hearer to be convinced of its truth. Searle, "A Taxonomy of Illocutionary Acts," 13.

[9] Searle, *Rationality in Action*, 173.

[10] H. P. Grice, "The Causal Theory of Perception," *Proceedings of the Aristotelian Society* 35 (1961): 124–26.

[11] J. L. Austin, "Other Minds," in *Philosophical Papers* (Oxford; New York: Oxford University Press, 1979), 82.

[12] Searle, *Speech Acts*, 28.

[13] Gustavo Faigenbaum, *Conversations with John Searle* (Montevideo, Uruguay: Libros en Red, 2003), 181.

CHAPTER 8: THE CONSTRUCTION OF SOCIAL REALITY

[1] No theorist disagrees with this basic claim. The semanticist only maintains that while words are *typically* uttered with the intention of doing something (pragmatics), they count as linguistic in virtue of the fact that they represent the world as being a certain way (semantics; conditions of satisfaction). Thus the semanticist maintains that an utterance may be meaningful, even when the speaker lacks the intention of producing any illocutionary or perlocutionary effect. Also, as noted in the last chapter, the ultimate function or purpose of the utterance is typically found in the perlocutionary intention.

[2] In *The Construction of Social Reality* Searle recommends that the characterization of speech acts as "conventional" or "arbitrary" is more misleading than helpful. Searle, *The Construction of Social Reality*, 28. Obviously some actions are ill-suited to count as, say, a speech act, given the purposes to which they tend. High frequency noises above the auditory range of humans cannot, at least in practice, be used to communicate. Common pebbles will not be used as a medium of exchange. The descriptors "conventional" and "arbitrary," while driving at an important feature of the institutional, misrepresent the fact that there are substantial physical constraints placed on the range of potential means.

[3] Ibid., 5–6.

[4] Ibid., 36, 57.

[5] Ibid., 97.

[6] Ibid., 135.

[7] Joshua Rust, *John Searle and the Construction of Social Reality*, Continuum Studies in American Philosophy (London; New York: Continuum, 2006), 15–16.

[8] Searle, *The Construction of Social Reality*, 70.

[9] Christopher Marquis, "Absent from the Korea Talks: Bush's Hard-Liner," *New York Times*, September 2, 2003.

[10] Ibid.

[11] Searle writes, "the statement 'I now have a pain in my lower back' reports an epistemically objective fact in the sense that it is made true by the existence of an actual fact that is not dependent on any stance, attitudes, or opinions of observers. However, the phenomenon itself, the actual pain, has a subjective mode of existence." Searle, *The Construction of Social Reality*, 9.

[12] Ibid., 2.
[13] Ibid., 9.
[14] Ibid., 97.
[15] Note that this argument parallels the connection principle, wherein something counts as intentional if it *could* be made conscious; this is not an accident. The deontic rules which constitute institutional facts have a derived intentionality. Thus, Searle has to maintain that they exist somewhere, even when they are not explicitly codified. Uncodified rules are subconscious in the sense that they could be made conscious or explicit.
[16] Searle, *The Construction of Social Reality*, 88.
[17] Alasdair C. MacIntyre, *After Virtue: A Study in Moral Theory*, 3rd ed. (Notre Dame, Ind.: University of Notre Dame Press, 2007), 152.
[18] For a more precise exhibition of this criticism see Rust, *John Searle and the Construction of Social Reality*, 138–82.

CHAPTER 9: TOPICS CONCERNING INSTITUTIONAL REALITY: REASONS, LANGUAGE, POLITICS, AND THE BACKGROUND

[1] Note that for Davidson "action" refers to behavior, but only those behaviors which happen to be caused by intentional states. For Searle "action" refers to both the behavior and the intentional states.
[2] Searle, *Rationality in Action*, 118–19.
[3] Ibid., 37–38.
[4] It should be noted that the Classical Model can make room for desire-independent reasons. Davidson remains open to this possibility. Davidson's notion of a proattitude is similar to Searle's notion of a motivator, in that it includes not just desires but duties and obligations. Searle nevertheless criticizes Davidson for overstating the analogy between desires and other kinds of motivators. Similar remarks apply to Bernard Williams' conception of a motivational set S. Ibid., 169–70.
[5] Ibid., 178–79; John R. Searle, "How to Derive 'Ought' From 'Is'," in *Concepts in Social & Political Philosophy*, ed. Richard E. Flathman (New York: Macmillan, 1973).
[6] Wittgenstein, *Philosophical Investigations*, §2.
[7] Searle, "How to Derive 'Ought' From 'Is'."
[8] Ibid., 56.
[9] Searle, *The Construction of Social Reality*, 100.
[10] Searle, "How to Derive 'Ought' From 'Is'," 57.
[11] Note that in "How to Derive an 'Ought' from an 'Is'," Searle appears to deny that all descriptions or assertives have a deontological component. Ibid., 58.
[12] This articulation misses the fact that some speech acts, such as directives ("Block!"), can impose rights and obligations, not just on a speaker but on the hearer as well. Searle, *Rationality in Action*, 173.
[13] Ibid., 185.
[14] Ibid., 174.
[15] Ibid., 180.

¹⁶ The details of this remarkable claim are not spelled out clearly in *Rationality in Action*. In what sense am I so bound? That is, in what sense can I *not* be indifferent to the truth of my own assertions? Prima facie, this seems to imply that it is somehow impossible for an asserter to lie, depending on how we understand the sense in which a speaker is bound to the truth of their statements. Searle's claim seems stronger than Timothy Williamson's claim that knowledge is the norm for assertion (that is, in asserting a speaker *ought* to know of and so believe in what they speak) in that the former is putting forth belief as a condition for the possibility of assertion. My obligation to move the bishop on the diagonal is not simply a norm for playing chess; it is a condition for chess's possibility. Ibid., 180–81. Timothy Williamson, *Knowledge and its Limits* (Oxford; New York: Oxford University Press, 2000), 238–69.

¹⁷ Searle, *The Construction of Social Reality*, 71.

¹⁸ Searle, *Freedom and Neurobiology.*

¹⁹ Ibid., 95–97, 108.

²⁰ Ibid., 100.

²¹ Hacking writes that "Social constructionists about *X* tend to hold that: (1) *X* need not have existed, or need not be at all as it is. *X*, or *X* as it is at present, is not determined by the nature of things, it is not inevitable." Hacking, *The Social Construction of What?* 6.

²² Searle, *The Construction of Social Reality*, 132–37.

²³ Searle, *Intentionality*, 143.

²⁴ Ibid., 157.

²⁵ Searle, *The Construction of Social Reality*, 129.

²⁶ Ibid., 140.

²⁷ Ibid., 137.

²⁸ Van Fraassen, *The Scientific Image*, 141.

²⁹ Searle, *The Construction of Social Reality*, 145.

³⁰ Ibid., 142.

³¹ Ibid.

³² Searle's paradoxical remarks can be highlighted in a number of different ways depending on which of Searle's seemingly incompatible articulations of the Background are taken as more central. For a different argument, where I take seriously the notion that the Background is a category of neurophysiological causation, see Chapter 3 of Rust, *John Searle and the Construction of Social Reality*.

³³ Searle, *The Construction of Social Reality*, 28–29.

BIBLIOGRAPHY

Anscombe, G. E. M. *Intention*. Ithaca, N.Y.: Cornell University Press, 1957.

Austin, J. L. *How to Do Things with Words*, The William James Lectures; 1955. Cambridge, Mass.: Harvard University Press, 1962.

—"Other Minds." In *Philosophical Papers*, edited by J. O. Urmson and G. J. Warnock, 76–116. Oxford; New York: Oxford University Press, 1979.

Bach, Kent. "Speech Acts and Pragmatics." In *The Blackwell Guide to the Philosophy of Language*, edited by Michael Devitt and Richard Hanley, pp. 147–67, 446 pp. Malden, Mass.: Blackwell, 2006.

Barsoum, M. W., A. Ganguly, and G. Hug. "Microstructural Evidence of Reconstituted Limestone Blocks in the Great Pyramids of Egypt." *Journal of the American Ceramic Society* 89, no. 12 (2006): 3788–96.

Berkeley, George. *A Treatise Concerning the Principles of Human Knowledge*. Oxford; New York: Oxford University Press, 1998.

Chisholm, R. M. "Freedom in Action." In *Freedom and Determinism*, edited by Keith Lehrer, pp. 11–44. New York: Random House, 1966.

Davidson, Donald. "Actions, Reasons, and Causes." In *Essays on Actions and Events*, pp. 3–20, 324 pp. Oxford; New York: Clarendon Press; Oxford University Press, 2001.

—"Freedom to Act." In *Essays on Freedom of Action*, edited by Ted Honderich, pp. 63–81, 215 pp. London; Boston: Routledge and Kegan Paul, 1973.

—"Intending." In *Essays on Actions and Events*, pp. 83–102, 324 pp. Oxford; New York: Clarendon Press; Oxford University Press, 2001.

Dreyfus, Hubert L. *Being-in-the-World: A Commentary on Heidegger's Being and Time, Division I*. Cambridge, Mass.: MIT Press, 1991.

Faigenbaum, Gustavo. *Conversations with John Searle*. Montevideo, Uruguay: Libros en Red, 2003.

Feyerabend, Paul. "Mental Events and the Brain." *Journal of Philosophy* 40 (1963): 295–96.

Frankfurt, Harry G. *The Importance of What We Care about: Philosophical Essays*. Cambridge; New York: Cambridge University Press, 1988.

Frigg, Roman. "Re-presenting Scientific Representation." PhD dissertation; London School of Economics, (2003).

Goodman, Nelson. *Of Mind and Other Matters*. Cambridge, Mass.: Harvard University Press, 1984.

Grice, H. P. "The Causal Theory of Perception." *Proceedings of the Aristotelian Society* 35, (1961): 121–53.

—"Meaning." *The Philosophical Review* 66, no. 3 (1957): 377–88.
—*Studies in the Way of Words.* Cambridge, Mass.: Harvard University Press, 1989.
Hacking, Ian. *The Social Construction of What?* Cambridge, Mass.: Harvard University Press, 1999.
Hanna, Robert. *Kant, Science, and Human Nature.* Oxford; New York: Clarendon Press; Oxford University Press, 2006.
Jackson, Frank. *From Metaphysics to Ethics: A Defence of Conceptual Analysis.* Oxford; New York: Clarendon Press; Oxford University Press, 1998.
—"What Mary Didn't Know." *The Journal of Philosophy* 83, no. 5 (1986): 291.
Kant, Immanuel. *Critique of Pure Reason,* translated by Paul Guyer and Allen W. Wood. Cambridge; New York: Cambridge University Press, 1998.
Kenneally, Christine. *The First Word: The Search for the Origins of Language.* New York: Viking, 2007.
Kuhn, Thomas S. *Structure of Scientific Revolutions.* 3rd ed. Chicago, Ill.: The University of Chicago Press, 1962.
MacIntyre, Alasdair C. *After Virtue: A Study in Moral Theory.* 3rd ed. Notre Dame, Ind.: University of Notre Dame Press, 2007.
Marquis, Christopher. "Absent from the Korea Talks: Bush's Hard-Liner." *New York Times,* September 2, 2003.
Moore, G. E. "Proof of an External World." In *Philosophical Papers,* pp. 127–50. London; New York: Allen & Unwin; Macmillan, 1959.
Nagel, T. "What Is It like to Be a Bat?" *The Philosophical Review* 83, no. 4 (1974): 435.
Nietzsche, Friedrich Wilhelm. *The Will to Power,* edited by Walter Arnold Kaufmann and R. J. Hollingdale. New York: Random House, 1967.
Papineau, David. "Power and Consciousness on the Clapham Omnibus." *Times Online* (2008), http://entertainment.timesonline.co.uk/tol/arts_and_entertainment/the_tls/article3196720.ece (Last accessed on October 2, 2008.)
Pickering, Andrew. *Constructing Quarks: A Sociological History of Particle Physics.* Chicago, Ill.: University of Chicago Press, 1984.
Pitt, David. "Mental Representation." In *The Stanford Encyclopedia of Philosophy,* edited by Edward N. Zalta, 2008. http://plato.stanford.edu/entries/mental-representation/(Last accessed date September 25, 2008).
Place, U. T. "Is Consciousness a Brain Process?" *British Journal of Psychology* 47 (1956): 44–50.
Putnam, Hilary. "Why There Isn't a Ready-Made World." *Synthese* 51, no. 2 (1982): 141–67.
Ramsey, William. "Prototypes and Conceptual Analysis." In *Rethinking Intuition: The Psychology of Intuition and Its Role in Philosophical Inquiry,* edited by Michael R. DePaul and William Ramsey, pp. 161–78, 335 pp. Lanham, Md.: Rowman & Littlefield, 1998.
Rorty, R. "Mind-Body Identity, Privacy and Categories." *Review of Metaphysics* 19, no. 1 (1965): 24.
Russell, Bertrand. *The Philosophy of Logical Atomism,* edited by David Francis Pears. LaSalle, Ill.: Open Court, 1985.

—*The Problems of Philosophy*. Mineola, N.Y.: Dover, 1999.

Rust, Joshua. *John Searle and the Construction of Social Reality*, Continuum Studies in American Philosophy. London; New York: Continuum, 2006.

Schiffer, Stephen R. *Meaning*. Oxford: Clarendon Press, 1972.

Searle, John R. "The Chinese Room." In *The MIT Encyclopedia of the Cognitive Sciences*, edited by R. A. Wilson and F. Keil, pp. 115–16. Cambridge, Mass.: MIT Press, 1999.

—*The Construction of Social Reality*. New York: The Free Press, 1995.

—*Freedom and Neurobiology: Reflections on Free Will, Language, and Political Power*, Columbia Themes in Philosophy. New York: Columbia University Press, 2007.

—"How Performatives Work." *Linguistics and Philosophy* 12 (1989): 535–58.

—"How to Derive 'Ought' from 'Is'." *The Philosophical Review*, 73 (1964): 43–58.

—*Intentionality*. Cambridge: Cambridge University Press, 1983.

—"The Limits of Phenomenology." In *Essays in Honor of Hubert L. Dreyfus*, edited by Hubert L. Dreyfus, Mark A. Wrathall and J. E. Malpas, pp. 71–92. Cambridge, Mass.: MIT Press, 2000.

—"Meaning, Communication, and Representation." In *Philosophical Grounds of Rationality: Intentions, Categories, Ends*, edited by Richard E. Grandy and Richard Warner, pp. 209–26. Oxford: Clarendon Press, 1986.

—*Mind, Language, and Society: Philosophy in the Real World*. New York: Basic Books, 1998.

—*Mind: A Brief Introduction*. Oxford; New York: Oxford University Press, 2004.

—"A Philosophical Self-Portrait." In *The Penguin Dictionary of Philosophy*, edited by Thomas Mautner, 512–14. London; New York: Penguin Books, 1997.

—*Rationality in Action*. Cambridge, Mass.: The MIT Press, 2001.

—*The Rediscovery of the Mind*. Cambridge, Mass.: MIT Press, 1992.

—*Speech Acts*. Cambridge: Cambridge University Press, 1969.

—"A Taxonomy of Illocutionary Acts." In *Expression and Meaning: Studies in the Theory of Speech Acts*, pp. 1–29, 187 pp. Cambridge; New York: Cambridge University Press, 1979.

—"Toward a Unified Theory of Reality." *Harvard Review of Philosophy* 12 (2004): 93–135.

—"What Is to Be Done?" *Topoi* 25 (2006): 101–08.

Sellars, Wilfrid. *Philosophy and the Scientific Image of Man*, edited by Robert Garland Colodny, Frontiers of Science and Philosophy. Pittsburgh, Pa.: University of Pittsburgh Press, 1962.

Shaffer, Michael J. "Bayesian Confirmation of Theories That Incorporate Idealizations." *Philosophy of Science* 68, no. 3 (2001): 36–52.

Smart, J. J. C. "Sensations and Brain Processes." *The Philosophical Review* 68, no. 2 (1959): 141.

Stalnaker, Robert. "Assertion." In *Context and Content: Essays on Intentionality in Speech and Thought*, pp. 78–96, 283 pp. Oxford; New York: Oxford University Press, 1999.

Strawson, P. F. "Meaning and Truth." In *Logico-Linguistic Papers*, 251 p. London: Methuen, 1971.

Turing, Alan M. "Computing Machinery and Intelligence." *Mind*, no. 54 (1950): 433–57.

van Fraassen, Bas C. *The Scientific Image*. Oxford; New York: Clarendon Press; Oxford University Press, 1980.

Williamson, Timothy. *Knowledge and Its Limits*. Oxford; New York: Oxford University Press, 2000.

Wittgenstein, Ludwig. *Blue and Brown Books*. New York: Perennial, 1942.

—*On Certainty*, translated by G. E. M. Anscombe and G. H. von Wright. New York: Harper, 1969.

—*Philosophical Investigations*, translated by G. E. M. Anscombe. 3rd ed. New Jersey: Prentice-Hall, 1958.

—*Tractatus Logico-Philosophicus*, edited by David Francis Pears and Brian McGuinness, Routledge Classics. London; New York: Routledge, 2001.

Wright, Larry. *Critical Thinking*. Oxford: Oxford University Press, 2001.

—*Teleological Explanations: An Etiological Analysis of Goals and Functions*. Berkeley, Calif.: University of California Press, 1976.

INDEX